D1827548

EMOTIONAL EATING

Feeding Your Feelings

By

Aron Smith

DEDICATION

To everyone out there feeling hurt, lost or alone, and trying their best to make things better

Table of Contents

INTRODUCTION

Sometimes you feel hurt, angry, betrayed, lost or out of place. You feel like it's just you against the world. Like no one understands what you are going through. You feel like the pain of whatever you are going through will last forever. Like you are choking on something and you can't get enough air.

Trust me, we have all felt like that at some point in our lives.

It could be any situation causing these feelings. Whether you are dealing with work issues, juggling your relationships, and dealing with your **very** jealous financial issues equally screaming for your attention on the sidelines.

Remember that moment when someone called you fat? *I am sure you can't forget.* When someone insulted you and made you feel worthless. When the man or woman you loved broke up with you when you felt everything was going alright. When someone disappointed you, yelled at you or pissed you off. Or when you just lost your job. All you wanted was to be left on your own at that moment to wallow in self-pity, to nurse your broken heart. You wanted something that could soothe you and calm you.

Or something to punch!

At that moment, you started to crave certain foods or snacks that would make you feel better. Foods you believe can change any bad mood into a good one. You just want to curl up on your favorite couch and take up a box of chocolates, ice cream, chips or hot cheesy pizza from your favorite pizza store.

That there, is you using food to comfort yourself and deal with your issues. It's called **emotional eating.** It's also called stress eating. *Yes, there's such a thing.*

While some people consume moderate to large amounts of food during these times, when not done repeatedly, emotional eating is not considered serious enough to be termed an "eating disorder. " But! It can quickly and easily progress into that if a person is not careful. Now, isn't that discouraging?

Some people will ask why it's a problem to eat what you want, or to eat something that makes you feel good about yourself. Well, the answer is while it might feel good, it is not necessarily good for you.

Take for instance an obese person having little or no control over what they eat and how much they eat because they want to feel good. I am sure we all know the health risks that come with being obese. Or can you imagine a diabetic patient having an uncontrollable craving for sugary confections?
We all know how that will end.

This issue is not gender specific or even age specific. It happens to a lot of people worldwide, round the clock. There's always an unending stream of **comfort eaters.** The question is why?

The most important thing to understand about comfort eating is food is not just a source of nourishment for our body. It is also quite connected with our emotions. The connection between the food we eat and our emotions is one that has been set since the day we were born. That is why a baby can bring the roof down when hungry, then go back to being an angelic specimen when satisfied.

Psychologists say that is why children are more likely to repeat a good deed if they've been rewarded for doing it before, in the hopes of getting that cookie or candy again. So, as they grow, they unconsciously do these things even when there might not be a physical reward, because they have conditioned themselves to respond that way.

Chapter One

The Mentality

There are many misconceptions about emotional eating. For so long, people have believed emotional eating is **only** a result of low self-esteem, negative emotions and so on. What they do not know is people eat to express good emotions too, and not necessarily out of hunger. They just want to celebrate!

Amazing, right? There are happy people who are emotional eaters too!

When we talk about emotional eating, we mostly point the finger, recounting instances where someone else overate because they were sad, or had a bad divorce, or maybe even lost a loved one. That's wrong, because we have all at some point engaged in emotional eating! It may be surprising, but it's true!

Stop shaking your head. You have, too!

You ask me how? Well, I'll gladly remind you of those times in the summer when you feel so hot. You feel like you're about to spontaneously combust, and you desperately want to cool off any way you can. So you pass by that ice cream shop, buy a cone with a couple scoops, or three, because you worked out super-hard in the morning, so you've earned it. One bite and you sigh in bliss.

Yeah, I know, it's an awesome feeling.

Don't lie to yourself. You know it wasn't just that one time. If you try to remember, you would see you've found yourself doing this often. It may even have become a routine to deal with the heat. That, my friend, is emotional eating.

The major problem is many people have a hard time distinguishing between **true hunger** and **emotional hunger**. It's not really hard to differentiate between the two, actually. If you often find yourself chewing on something when you are not particularly hungry, especially if these foods you munch on are rich in sugar or carbs, then you most likely are eating emotionally.

Doesn't matter if you eat a lot of chocolate because it makes your cramps ease up, or if you eat hot, cheesy, stringy pizza every time you are trying to forget you are yet to meet a deadline at work, or you eat chips every time your butt is parked on the couch and you've got a front and center view of the TV. It's still emotional eating.

"Emotional eating? My food has feelings or what?"

"Emotional eating is just for chicks, right bros?"

Nope. A lot of guys even in this day and age believe emotional eating affects only women.

So wrong!

Like I said before, emotional eating is not gender or age specific. It can affect an older lady who is fighting boredom after hours of knitting, a teenage girl who wasn't noticed by her heartthrob, an adolescent male who messed up at a game, a middle-aged woman with an overly generous behind, or even an older guy insecure about his few extra pounds he needs to shed.

It can happen to anyone!

You might feel like you are an exception because you are on a diet. Surprisingly, people on diets are more prone to emotional eating. You know, they're trying not to eat too much of this, that, and the other, then suddenly something bad (or good) happens, and all those rules fly right out the window. Staying fit is hard! Losing weight is even harder. And in a few moments of weakness, you have a cookie and promise yourself it's going to be just the one. Next thing you know, you've turned into the Cookie Monster. "Me want cookie! Me eat cookie! Om nom nom nom!" Next thing you know, goodbye diet.

You might not even know you are doing this. It even feels like you can't help yourself because you crave this comfort food unconsciously. I know it is not easy. Thousands of people around the globe are going through the same right now!

Scientists to date are trying to figure out why people engage in emotional eating when it inevitably leads to regrets. Many people make a conscious effort not to eat to soothe frayed nerves or hurt feelings, and when that fails despite their best efforts, they start to feel guilty.

People on diets feel like they have betrayed themselves and sabotaged their efforts. This leads to self-recrimination, and in some severe cases depression, because they have pushed themselves further away from achieving their goal.

Imagine trying to lose postnatal weight., and then - like most women - you suffer postnatal depression, so you indulge in emotional eating. Of course after you have realized the implications of your actions, you become further depressed as instead of losing weight like you planned, you end up piling it on.

The problem is comfort foods don't actually help you handle your emotional problems. The euphoric feeling you get are very temporary. That brief high you get is quickly replaced by deep feelings of guilt, which leads to more consumption of comfort foods. And so the cycle continues.

Emotional Eating and The Dopamine Rush

I need to say this right now: Don't be too harsh on yourself if you're an emotional eater! Some very delicious foods trigger the production of a chemical in the brain called **dopamine.** It is also referred to as a "feel-good" chemical. So, once you consume certain foods or sugary confections, it triggers a euphoric feeling which makes you feel like a conqueror. You feel like you could fly and touch the sun. Never mind that the sun would totally incinerate you. Fascinating, right?

Back to Earth!

It so happens this feeling of euphoria lasts only three minutes. ***Three minutes!*** Three minutes of being on Cloud Nine, and endless hours of never-ending agony and self-recrimination.

Some people think different people seek comfort from the same foods. That is wrong. There are a number of people who do not like sugary foods. Different people from different cultural groups and countries have different comfort foods. What works for Michelle may not work for Mitchell.

Where's The Off Switch?

All this might seem mind boggling. I mean it's just food, right? Why do we need to overanalyze eating, for goodness sake? We need food to survive! Yes, I understand. But emotional eating is a real problem that needs to be dealt with. It's not your eating. It's your feelings demanding to be fed!

Then how do I stop it? You want to know. Rightfully so.

You can't! You just can't! It's not a switch to be turned on and off on a whim. It's more than that! We are talking about your feelings,. The essence of you. We're talking about what makes you human! You're probably thinking there's no point to reading this book since you can't stop eating emotionally anyway. Don't put it down just yet. There's hope. I promise. You just need to first understand what it is you are going through.

We are going to find out, so stay tuned.

No, not with a bowl of chips!

Chapter Two

The Science Behind Eating Emotionally

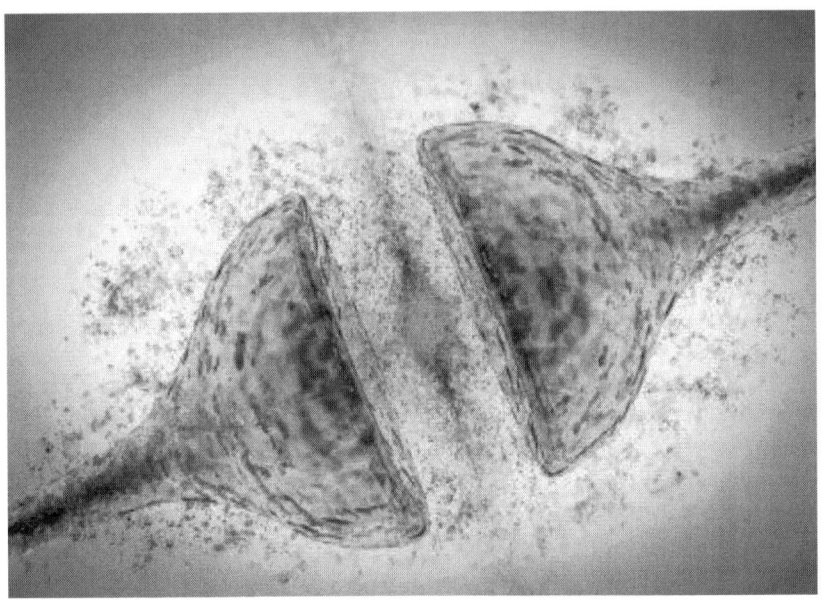

A random, science-y picture for... Science!

Emotional eating can be a serious problem if left unchecked. It can lead to food addiction and some other eating disorders. Physically, it might sabotage all your weight loss plans and lead to obesity. You may get a very generous behind and a minivan in the front.

Like I mentioned before, **dopamine** is a chemical which gives you all the feel-good feels. It's a neurotransmitter, which, as the name implies, transmits signals to the brain. It is responsible for motivation, memory, and behavior. When hard drugs are abused, guess what happens? The floodgates are opened, and you get that dopamine rush.

There is a connection between the midbrain and the forebrain which is an important evolutionary site for pleasure and addiction. **Dopamine** is known to activate the **hippocampus**. This is a site for learning and storage in the brain. Think of it this way: if it is registered in your brain that pizza gives you joy or soothes you, it is likely you will be found at Pizza Hut more often than not, just because.

Interesting research has discovered that in comparison to women within the healthy weight range, women above the healthy weight range have more activities going on in the **mesolimbic** part of the brain when presented with images of pizza, in comparison to other kinds of foods like bread.

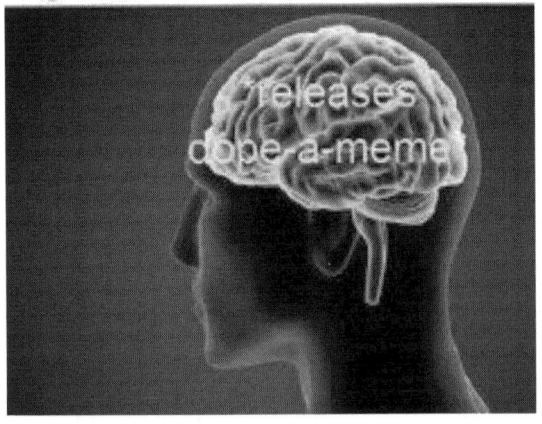

Dopamine is responsible for that rush of euphoria you feel when you are sitting with a bowl of ice cream in front of the TV watching the games. *Yes, dopamine is dope, I mean!* See what I did there? I should stop writing and go be a rapper.

Another key thing to consider is **cortisol.** It is a stress hormone which balances some nutrients in our bodies, such as the macronutrients - carbohydrates, fats and proteins. When you are all wound up or overworked, your bloodstream is flooded with cortisol, which leads to an uncontrollable craving for sugary confections, salty chips or very cheesy pizza.

Let's Talk Hormones

Cortisol is Batman. Know who Robin is? His righthand man, **serotonin.** Serotonin also called the "happy chemical." It is naturally not found in the food we eat, but **tryptophan**, an amino acid, plays a huge part in the production of **serotonin.**

Hormones like serotonin and **glutamate** are responsible for the brain's reward system. Serotonin reduces stress and lightens mood. Glutamate affects response to environmental stimuli. This is the reason emotional or physical stress bring about an intense craving for the abused substance, or food. It's also why relapses are so common.

We are more likely to fall back into addiction if we are under a lot of pressure or revert back to the situation which brought about the genesis of the addiction. The **dopamine** system is not a bed of roses. *Actually, it is.* It certainly feels that way. Just remember: *roses have thorns*!

There is a pre-installed negative feedback function. Increasing use or overuse of the **dopamine** system reduces the gross number of **dopamine** receptors available. This explains the ideology of tolerance. Basically, we require more and more of the misused substance to stimulate our currently lacking **dopamine** receptors. Take the average marijuana user. In the beginning, it's easy for them to feel high. Over time, with repetitive use, they need more than they used to before they can feel the same level of high as in the beginning.

Research has shown adults with lower **dopamine** levels are most likely to have a high body mass index. This shows they required more food to produce **dopamine,** which resulted in the weight gain. It may all seem complicated, but trust me it is not.

Once you start consuming these foods out of want and no longer out of need, the production of **dopamine** and **cortisol** go on autopilot. This means, unlike before, your body doesn't produce these hormones even when absolutely necessary.

Now, you just have to think of a food, look at it somewhere, smell it, and you have an uncontrollable craving to eat it. You need to have your fix! Once an individual has lost control of their eating habits, eating can easily turn into an addiction. You become a food addict. *Food addiction is a serious issue!*

Food addiction can have very serious consequences, some are even fatal. It may lead to obesity, high cholesterol levels, diabetes, hypertension, and other serious health problems. Those are just the tamer stuff I listed. There are problems even worse!

We have to be careful of what we eat and how we eat. Ultimately, it's not about how you live, but how well you live. We all want good lives but it's up to us to take responsibility. And to take charge of our stomachs!

Chapter Three

The Psychology of Emotional Eating

When we improve on the types of foods we consume, we will most likely be able to control certain involuntary impulses and cravings, and manage our weight better. Did you know the way your day plays out is determined by what you eat? *You really are what you eat.* That's not just a cliché. It's true.

When you do not eat enough or you consume too much food, it can seriously affect your health and your way of life. This might paint a morbid image of food in your mind, but don't let it. Remember, balance is key. That's why people are less likely to eat foods which have caused them to vomit. A person is less likely to retry the food for fear of repeating the experience.

Who's the Boss? Your Head, or Your Stomach?

You have to be in control of your body and your mind. You have to be the dominant character when making food choices and not your feelings. When you are in control, you are more likely to make an effort to cut back on foods you know present a serious risk to your health.

If you leave your feelings in charge, you will end up eating what feels good and kills slowly. You'll wind up like a huge whale with a ticking time bomb in it.

While we always have it at the back of our minds to eat healthy, stay hydrated, and sleep well, all this is often easier said than done. It's like a very vivid dream you have and then forget when you wake up. Keep in mind the keyword here is will. Will! As in the driving need to fulfill a set goal. *Not will, as in Will.I.Am.*

Psychology and Emotional Eating

You might wonder what psychology has to do with emotional eating. Well, psychology studies human behavior. It studies why humans act the way they do. For people trying to find a way to manage emotional eating, psychology will help. How?

- **It addresses your character.** Your eating behaviors and patterns would need to be observed so an action plan **tailored to your needs** can be designed.

- **You can identify your thought patterns.** Your thoughts and emotions would need to be analyzed. You can then discover what your emotional triggers are. Once your cognitive pattern has been thoroughly explored with the help of a licensed professional, they can then figure out a fitting solution to the problem.

The Road Ahead

The truth is no matter what solutions are proffered; they just won't work unless you're ready to make a change. You have to be willing to drop emotional eating and lead a healthier life. Your decision must be unwavering. This requires putting a lot of effort into achieving success, limiting distractions, and setting targets.

You also have to be self-aware. Become mindful. Do not act unconsciously. Just observe and watch for triggers that induce specific cravings. Then, be careful of what you eat and how much you do it.

Try replacing your sugary confections with something sugary, but healthy. Like an apple, or pineapple. Whenever you start to have your cravings for a pastry, try to replace is with something healthier. It won't be easy, but where there's a will, there's a way. How do you get the will? **Find your why.** When you have solid, concrete reasons for wanting to make a change, you'll find the "how" gets that much more achievable.

There is nothing more satisfying than looking back at some mistakes you have made and seeing that you have overcome them. Yes, the past may have shaped your undesirable present. But the present shapes the future, every moment you spend wallowing in self-pity, body shaming yourself, and languishing in the throes of a broken heart, just keeps you from achieving the final goal.

If you stick with me, I'm going to give you the tools you need to overcome your emotional eating. You just have to decide that you can, and you will. Against all odds. It's no secret people tend to get what they want if they put their all into it.

So are you with me? I want you all in. I want you to remember why you started, whenever you want to quit. I want you to know I'm rooting for you. I want you to know I've seen countless people beat emotional eating. I've seen it happen, so I know it can be done. I know **you can do it.** But I can only hold your hand. You're going to have to put one foot in front of the other and take this journey with me. Can you do it? Will you do it?

Before you move on to the next chapter, I want you to ask yourself one thing.

Are you worth it?

Don't turn the page until you realize and feel deeply in your bones the only correct answer to that question.

Yes. You are worth it. So very worth it.

Chapter Four

At War With Food?

War has been declared. Swords have been drawn. *Time to battle!*

You might be wondering how you can be at war with food. We're going to get into that right now. See, as an emotional eater, there is constant war between your will and your cravings. Every single time you saw the cravings win and you were helpless to stop it? Those were squabbles compared to what is coming.

Laying Siege!

A war has been declared and you are going to have to be your own knight in shining armor because this is a battle that mercenaries can't fight on your behalf. Every failed attempt you have had with dealing with your emotional eating has brought you closer to this moment of decision.

When your emotions start to get frayed as a response to negative stimuli, you can take measures to control your cravings. More often than not, you will indulge in emotional eating when you are at your weakest emotionally.

Go Do Something ELSE!
I don't care what it is, as long as it's not eating, and it's not going to kill you. Listen to some music. Listen to a TED Talk or some podcast or something. Talk to some friends. Go out. Go jog. Cycle. Do anything **but** eat at that moment.

Here's why.

Hunger and Cravings Come In Waves

If you've always just given in to all your cravings, chances are you've never noticed hunger actually comes in waves. It's not something that hits you full on and just keeps getting worse until you finally shove something into your piehole.

Me: "I'm so hungry"
Friend: "didn't u just eat"
Me:
That wasn't me. That was Patricia.

Your hunger actually comes in waves. So do your cravings. If you can wait them out, then that's more than half the battle! But how exactly do you ride the wave of your cravings without actually giving in? See the previous section. **Do something else.** If you're busy, if you give your mind something else to focus on, then chances are it will not be thinking about what next to eat.

Are You In Denial?

One of the hardest things ever is fixing the results caused by a problem you created. If you're going to beat this thing, then the first step is acknowledging you actually have a problem.

Some people do not believe they have a problem. Especially when they believe they are eating "well." This happens when they rationalize it with various thoughts, like wanting to have a fuller figure, or to fill out their cheeks so they're no longer sunken. But then what happens when they successfully achieve those goals? *They just. Won't. Stop. Eating!* It won't be a pretty sight once your behind gets more *generous.*

If you've read up to this point and you're still trying to suss out whether or not you actually have a food problem, be honest with yourself. This is why it is a war. A battle of wills. Head versus stomach. Only the strongest man wins. You could always try weighing your options , but you don't have many. If you don't work now to stop your emotional eating habits, your self-esteem will be thrown into the mud and trod upon like so much **nothing**.

Fall In Love With Food

Wait... What? Yes, I said that. If you're at war with food, then that needs to end NOW. It's not food you need to be at war with. It's your own emotions. It's all the temptations which call to you, asking you to eat one more cookie, one more slice, one more forkful.

How do you fix this? **Love food that treats you good.** Imagine you're in a relationship with someone, and no matter how much you love them, they always make you feel like such utter crap. What do you do then? Of COURSE you ditch them!

So why are you still in a love affair with foods that treat you like shit? Yes, I cussed. I did that to snap you out of it. You know you feel like crap when you eat them. So fall in love with the good stuff instead! This way, you get rid of the guilt that keeps you trapped in the cycle of emotional eating. I'm not asking you to go on a diet. I'm asking you to fall in love with food worth loving. I'm asking you to love your body and treat it better. It's not going to be easy, but you can lean on friends and family. You can seek out professional help. I know you'll pull through!

Temptations

The main factor in emotional eating is the presence of temptation. If you know there is anything that might cause you to relapse into old habits, remove it. If it seems too much for you then flee!
There is no cowardice in retreat. You go to fight another day, bolder and stronger. I don't care if people laugh at you because of how fast you bolt out the room when someone walks in with a box of pizza. Do whatever you have to. Slowly and steadily you will win the battle.

Restrictive Dieting and Emotional Eating

For a lot of people, emotional eating is just a part of a wheel or a cycle formed from restrictive dieting.

You see, people are of the very wrong impression that it is only people who do not eat a lot when they are hungry that become emotional eaters. This misconception is why a lot of people are caught up in this vicious cycle. First they eat. Then they feel guilty for eating. To deal with the shame, they eat again. Wash, rinse, and repeat.

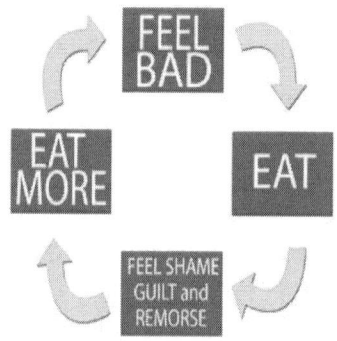

This is a cycle that has to be broken! It is a cycle of shame and self-derision!

Is it just me, or is it the food?

Over the years, food addiction has become a topic of interest among scientists. These scientists have come up with theories that state that foods rich in sugar, fat and salt are addictive, and they act upon the brain like some hard drugs such as cocaine!

The crazy thing is, the normal treatment for addiction is withdrawal and abstinence. That sure can't happen with food because we need it to survive.

Other researchers have asserted it may not be the food that is addictive, but it's more likely the individual who is prone to addiction. They propose it's the continuous cycle of shame and indulgence that creates addictive dependence, not the food itself.

If your emotional eating has progressed to a full blown addiction to food, then you have to try as much as possible not to bring your comfort food to your comfort zone. If you do, that's asking for trouble! One can't be too careful. The fact you are not a coward doesn't mean you should test your will unnecessarily.

Let's be real for a second here. You wouldn't leave a pyromaniac around a box of matches and some gasoline, would you? Then why would you allow all sorts of foods you **know** you're helplessly addicted to when you're trying to beat this thing?

Exactly.

Chapter Five

What Kind of Eater Are You?

What kind of foods are you often found eating? Your daily eating pattern can determine what kind of eater you are.

Are you usually found eating pork roast at dinner, or a bowl of fresh veggies? Are you more of a Mac and cheese person? All these speak volumes about the kind of eater you are if you are not yet aware of it.

Are your foods almost always paper wrapped from a fast food joint? Do you almost always eat while watching the games, chick flick or a horror movie? Have you always seen your self-accepting free food? Have you ever found yourself eating even when there is no gnawing hunger in your belly?

If you fit any of the descriptions given above, then you have most likely developed an unhealthy eating habit or pattern. Habits that will eventually sabotage every weight loss program you might have.

A lot of times, it is very simple to identify bad eating habits. Like when food becomes the only solution to your problems, or when it becomes the only stress relief method you can think of. When you start to think it is impossible that anything but food could make you better at that point. Sometimes, these signs are not clear enough so a person can go for a long time in ignorant bliss. Sometimes these habits become so much a part of you, you do not even realize you are doing them. They become unconscious actions. Dictated by your cravings and not your mind.

There are various types of eating habits and they vary from person to person. Experts have asserted these patterns are determined mostly by a person's behavior. With the majority of affected people being overweight or obese.

Stress Eating

You may notice you eat a bit more when you are stressed, but you won't always associate it with emotional eating. Especially when you are always munching on small things, which add up to become bigger things by the end of your day at work or school.

My job helps pay for the stress-eating caused by my job.

someecards

copingskills socialwork
socialworker socialworkhumor
socialworkproblems

Some people are always in a panic about what to eat and how to eat it. Most times because they find it difficult making a choice, they end up at the local restaurant, eating something oily and salty. This develops into a very unhealthy lifestyle. Because as is human nature, we always go for the simplest option in a time of confusion.

Task Eating

The type of eating pattern people are less likely to discover they have is **task eating**. People who always work easier with a bit of something in their mouths. Maybe a bit of chocolate while doing the laundry, some chips while cooking, a bit of gum while writing or even some soda while reading. People don't tend to notice this habit because the mind is occupied with the more important and difficult of the two tasks, the other just being the dormant of the two activities.

Multitasking!

Sometimes, people also eat because they're lonely. If this is you, you eat when you're alone. You eat to fill the void inside. That's really the only reason you're reaching for that 5th slice of pizza, even though your gut started to protest at slice 3.

This is not just some made up thing. Research shows there is a high likelihood for binge eaters to always feel lonely. This lonely eater has more fat than the rest of society, and tends to each at very odd, irregular times. Did you know loneliness actually stresses you out? Go figure!

Excuses, and How to Beat Them

We all know fast foods are known for their high fat and sugar or salt content, yet some people would rather eat fast food than eat healthy.

After all it's fast!

They do not want to sacrifice the time needed to buy some of the groceries and then to cook. Some give the excuse they do not know how to cook and yet there are healthier food options out there.

You have to keep note of your eating habits, so as to make it easier to find a solution to help yourself. Once you have discovered that the flesh is weak, but the mind is willing, you have to put measures to ensure you do not fall back into temptation.

Okay Aron, What Do I DO?

- Clear out that stash of chips you have in your cabinet.
- Buy some veggies and low calorie foods to store in your fridge, so you do not have a reason to drive out to that grocery store.
- If munching on something crunchy helps soothe you or relax you, try a healthy alternative like carrots! They're just as crunchy as chips, and so much better for you.

So, why did you just make that face?

"But Aron! It's not the same thing! It's not **my** thing!" Well do you want to be healthy or not? Then you have to learn to fall in love with the good stuff! Being and staying healthy should be *everybody's* thing!

Feeling Discouraged?

Now, you're probably thinking this is not worth the time and effort you're going to have to put in. But when people say, "This is not worth it," what they're really saying is **I am not worth it.** So I'm going to ask you again, are you, or are you not worth good health? Do you deserve it or not?

I said you are not just going to quit right off the bat. I already mentioned there is no off switch. So what's going to happen is you are going to wean yourself of these comfort foods. Since it's like a fix, quitting abruptly will do more harm than good.

You feel tired already? I know.

You will have to take it slowly. One step at a time. We will talk about how to do just that in the coming chapters. You just have to know you are not alone! You picked up this book for a reason. You picked it up because you know something's wrong. You've read this far because you're desperate for change. You'll get that change, but you're going to have to put in the work, amigo.

So it's time to deal with it. The best way to deal with something is to make sure you have all the facts.

You have to know your enemy. You have to make sure not to mistaken **emotional hunger** for **true hunger.**

We will talk about this in the next chapter.

Read on!

Chapter Six

Emotional Hunger Versus Physical Hunger

Right from infancy, we have been taught to identify hunger as the need for nourishment. The need for food. After all, food keeps us alive. The nutrients from food replace our worn out tissues. We know the basics of how the digestive system works. We learned we are to eat three square meals in a day to sustain ourselves. But that isn't even anywhere near the truth. Our ancestors never ate three meals a day. We weren't designed that way.

Now it's even worse, because we have so much junk food available on demand. There's at least two or three fast food joints around the corner. We're a society that's gone food crazy! We're always supersizing this or that. It's nuts!

So allow me at this point to address the difference between **TRUE physical hunger, and emotional hunger.** Because it's only when you understand the difference that you'll be able to better handle yourself the next time you think of hitting that Taco Bell again.

Physical Hunger

True physical hunger is when your body pressingly demands food. It's undeniable. You stomach feels like an empty black hole. You might get a touch dizzy or light-headed. Sometimes you get nauseous. You can't really focus on the task at hand. You get so easily irritated, like, "Why does the air smell like air? What the hell?"

At that moment you know you have to eat something, and the sooner you do it, the better too. In other words, physical hunger is something you actually feel. There are actually physical effects. None of it is in your head.

All this is made possible by a hormone called **ghrelin**. Ghrelin is secreted by the stomach, brain, pancreas, and the small intestine. While it's responsible for many things in the human body, for now, we are only interested in its function as the "**hunger hormone.**"

You see, ghrelin is what tells the brain you know you need to open your piehole and shove some damn pies in. It increases a person's appetite and food absorption and is responsible for fat storage in humans.

When we are short of energy in the body, ghrelin is produced in the stomach walls, and then transmits a signal to the brain to increase appetite and food intake. It also plays a huge role in body mass.

Ghrelin has an arch nemesis called **leptin**. Who knew there was so much drama going on in your body, right? Anyway, leptin does the opposite of what ghrelin does. What's that? You guessed it. It reduces the appetite. Thin people are said to have lower amounts of ghrelin and higher leptin levels, while the reverse is the case for overweight people.

Those are the basics of physical hunger. So, next time your stomach growls, take it seriously because it's an emergency!

Emotional Hunger

Emotional hunger is all in your mind. Sometimes you might feel like you have a yawning ache inside you that nothing else can satisfy. Some might say what you are experiencing is emotional hunger. It is a very common thing to experience. Like we've mentioned before, it could even be that you're super excited about something and would like to celebrate with some food! Either way, emotional hunger can be really hard to beat, especially when you've indulged in it so much you now emotionally eat on autopilot. But you can beat it! Yo*u know, mind over matter!*

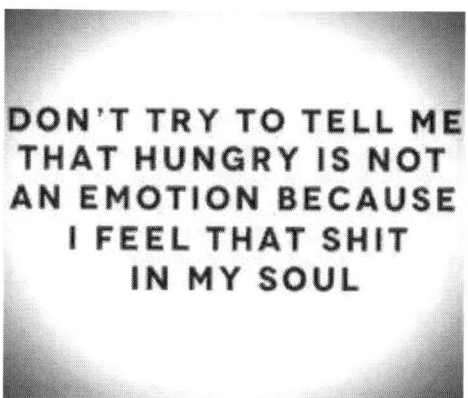

On Emotions

It's natural to feel emotions. That's a huge part of our schtick as humans. Emotions matter, and are important. You need to pay as much attention to them as you would the food you eat, or the job you do.

That is why we have to be cognizant of our habits and what issues cause us to be dependent on comfort foods. Once you are able to deal with the issues, give yourself a reality check. As a human, you have intelligence beyond compare. That level of intelligence gives you the ability to be a problem solver. But what good is intelligence without emotions? Even Siri has emotions! The emotions stop us from being totally robotic with needed attributes like empathy, compassion, love and the like.

Whatever it is you might have suffered emotionally; you can focus positive energy into getting better. It may just last longer than you want. But you will surely get better.

Emotional Hunger Triggers

Emotional hunger is easy to identify if you know what you are looking for. Have you been told by a friend or lover that you are too clingy? That you call too much? You have tried not to, but you can't seem to help yourself. Those are signs you are looking for emotional assurance. Signs you are afraid to be left alone.

When you act like this, you are more likely to read meanings where there are none. You feel hurt when people do not act the way you expect them to act or the way you envisioned them reacting. Once things don't go the way you planned, you go on an emotional decline which causes you to eat emotionally to satisfy your emotional hunger.

Because it feels like food is the only thing that doesn't judge you.

But it doesn't have to be so!

Overthinking

Emotionally hungry people are of the opinion they know what's in everybody's head, that they know what everybody is thinking and saying about them. Vying for acceptance among people and attention based solely out of the conclusions you have jumped to is a recipe for disaster. Why? When you get disappointed, your emotional belly is triggered, and next thing you know, you're three-quarters through a 1 liter tub of Ben and Jerry's.

One major characteristic of emotionally hungry people is trying to conform to certain ideologies or behaviors that have been deemed acceptable by a group of people so as not to be left out or hanging.

Self-Loathing and Dissatisfaction

More often than not, emotionally hungry people try to look, behave, talk or dress like other people. Mostly people with high profile social status. These people they want to have what the emotionally hungry person has tried unsuccessfully to get. A lot of friends, adoring fans, a great figure, six packs and muscles, a good job, an awesome ability to stick to diets, etc.

Most emotionally hungry people are often heard saying, "How I wish I could be like this person; she doesn't have to watch what she eats."
"How I wish I could look like that; I could wear whatever I wanted!" The more they wish, the sadder they become, and the weaker their resolve gets and the more they eat emotionally.
The whole concept of emotional hunger is the need to feel something different from the same old boring stuff. The need to "feel alive."

Ways People Deal with Emotional Hunger

While some eat emotionally to deal with these feelings, many others engage in more activities like sports to feel alive, and this in turn satisfies their emotional hunger. This is a great thing!

For others who crave human contact, they have sex - not necessarily to bond with the other person, but to feel whatever it is they want to feel. For most people, casual sex is completely acceptable. An emotionally hungry person will see it as more than just fun, though. To them, casual sex is a form of "nourishment." They avoid serious emotions that make them seem emotionally inadequate, choosing to go thrill seeking. This is them just trying to feel like they are good enough.

It's not their fault! In a purely judgmental society where a person can't be fit enough, slim enough, beautiful enough, or plainly good enough, they feel like they don't fit anywhere. Sex feels like the easiest way to make ourselves believe we have gotten our emotional hunger satisfied.

It's Not Enough Though

After some time, that too doesn't work or it feels like it doesn't work as well as it used to. At that moment we feel like we are getting approval from that one person we are interacting with. We feel we are good enough. We feel no other person's opinion matters. We feel we are worthy of another person's attention mixed with the "feel good" hormones secreted by the brain after sex. We seem satisfied at that moment and every other person's opinion seems inconsequential because we feel "good."

If you can relate, then you know chances are you are prone to having more sex partners than is healthy. Let's not even forget the fact there are enough STDs going around to get you in some hot water sooner or later. So when human contact becomes a less viable option, *hello emotional eating* - which, like I mentioned earlier, will set the wheel of shame and guilt on its course!

Sex and Emotional Pain

Although research has found sex eases the pain, sadness, and anger one feels against something; it's not exactly a long lasting solution to the underlying problem. While you can and should explore your sexuality in healthy ways, you should not be doing so as a way to cope with unhealthy emotions. Sadly, this is what the majority of people do. Research shows a majority of people who engage in random and casual sex are trying to feed an emotional hunger. Trying to prove they are good enough.

If you feel you can't go through recovering from emotional hunger on your own, you could always look for a trusted relative, or a friend. If you find despite the support systems you have available, beating this is a struggle, then don't be afraid or ashamed to seek out professional help.

Drugs and Emotional Hunger

Similar to sex, people turn to drug use as a coping mechanism for emotional hunger. This is very common in people who are trying to numb their pain. It may be the pain of loss, the pain of a broken home or even physical pain.

There a lot of short-term fixes people use when they do not know how to satisfy their emotional hunger. Some are very self-destructive methods, like drug abuse and alcohol. Others feel socially awkward so they would rather remain in isolation and adapt to their own company instead of interacting with others and risk being treated wrongly.

When you feel like you have lost all control of yourself. When you lose your ability to moderate your use of certain substances, or when you notice you are using these substances only to satisfy your emotional needs, it would be advisable to seek help from a therapist or doctor.

To most emotionally hungry people, the idea of being single or out of a relationship can be really scary. To avoid or lose that feeling of loneliness, you will most likely do things that are not good for your health. Things you feel will be able to fill that gaping emotional hole you are so scared of.

Emotional Hunger Triggered by Breakups

Most emotionally hungry people in relationships react very badly to an idea of a breakup. They never feel like there is a problem and most times refuse to believe they are the cause of the problem. These people have a very difficult time accepting rejection.

Since emotionally hungry people often seek acceptance and proximity with people, they usually do not know how to respect boundaries, because they find it difficult.

Dealing with emotional hunger is wholly about working with your mind, and reprogramming yourself to deal with issues in a healthier manner. Keep friends who are ready to invest as much energy into your relationship as you do.

So, we have ascertained that emotional hunger doesn't necessarily have to do with emotional eating all the time, but it can quickly progress into that if other methods of solace do not work for you.

Now, let's tackle this head on. I'm going to give you a step by step approach to dealing with emotional eating in the next chapter.

Chapter Seven

A Step-by-Step Guide to Eating Intelligently

If we want to live, then we have to eat. However, eating smart and healthy is something we need to train ourselves to do, especially in this day and age. Eating intelligently requires becoming conscious about what we eat.

We all know that what we eat and our health are in sync. The latter won't be possible without the former. Maintaining maximum health depends on what goes in through our mouths. Through what you eat, you take control of your life. Intelligent eating is a proactive measure with positive results. It's something that becomes a part of you, as you make the right choices one day at a time. Your body will thank you for it, and you'll be glad you decided to do this!

Eating intelligently is not about dieting in a particular way. It is modifying your normal eating habits for a better way of life. Intelligent eating, unlike some dietary plans, is a long-term project intended to maximize one's health and reduce the chances of illnesses. What I'm trying to say is I'm not offering you a weight loss program. I'm offering you the tools you need to improve the state of the mind and body. Intelligent eating is for people who are really interested in improving their health.

Quality Over Quantity

We must have heard constantly that food gives us energy and energy is required for us to be able to carry out our day to day activities. Eating intelligently requires a calculated approach at nourishment. You have to be able to eat well without eating too much or too less. You have to be able to eat at the right time without having to fast or skip meals.

Like I said in the beginning of the chapter, eating intelligently is in itself an art. Because, it takes a lot to be able to balance the right amount of fats, carbs, proteins and vitamins in a meal, after all, you can't go around carrying a scale. Everyone would doubt your sanity, you weirdo! Just kidding.

Your Brain and Glucose

Where food is concerned, the brain can be very selective. Like a petulant five year old with a sweet tooth, it loves simple sugar molecules. It loves glucose to be exact. And when the brain isn't provided with the glucose it needs, it gets really cranky and annoyed.

Since our bodies can easily produce glucose by breaking down carbohydrates, it would be right to conclude limiting carbs could reduce or impair cognitive function, right? Wrong. Your brain can actually function perfectly well on **ketones,** which are a byproduct of broken down fat. Some would argue it's even cleaner fuel for your brain, but this book isn't about that. The point is carbs are important, even if everyone wants to give them a bad rep. Just be sure to get the good sort in your belly! That means rather than have a burger or a bagel, you can opt for some whole wheat bread, or choose to have some wholegrain cereal other than the one that orange tiger Tony keeps pushing.

They're NOT!

Give your body the right stuff to work with, and you gradually stop craving all the bad stuff. Did you know the less sugar you take in, the less you crave? In fact, after long enough, it starts to taste just wrong!

So we're talking about eating intelligently, right? What would be the intelligent thing to do when you get a craving for cocaine's cousin Sugar? **Opt for foods with natural sugar in them.** Natural sugar is very good for our brains. Try as much as possible to include them as part of a balanced diet, with your meals, daily.

The Benefits of Intelligent Eating

There is so much to gain from fueling your body intelligently. You feel better, for starters. Your body's like a finely tuned engine. What do you think is going to happen if you fuel a Ferrari with Monster, instead of actually gas? Yeah, you can say goodbye to that 'rari now. It's gone.

The same thing applies to your body! If you wouldn't put the wrong fuel in your car, why treat your body any different or less!

When you give your body the right foods, when you choose to eat intelligently, what happens? You start to feel better. You start to **look better.** Your body is better able to fight disease, and to repair the damage all that junk food feasting powered by emotional hunger has done to you.

You get maximum energy. You're less bloated, and you have way less flatulence than you used to. If you suffer from Irritable Bowel Syndrome, the symptoms are lessened significantly.

Listen to Your Body Talk

No, I'm not talking about body language in conventional terms. I mean *pay attention to what your body is telling you.* Have you noticed that every time you drink something that has dairy in it, you tend to break out and you have horrible stomach cramps? **Then quit eating dairy for a bit.** Maybe a couple of weeks. Try it after the break, and if you notice you get the exact same reaction, guess what? You're lactose intolerant! So let go of the milk, and find other delicious alternatives.

Do you find you feel absolutely terrible every time you overeat? Aren't you sick of that? Listen, the only reason you feel that way is **because your body does not like that!** So what's the intelligent thing to do in this scenario? You could
- Chew slower
- Chew deliberately
- Put your fork down in between chews
- Sip some water every couple of minutes

Basically do anything to slow you down! This way, your brain is able to realize when you're full **before** you've eaten so much you look like Santa Claus.

Before you decide what to eat, ask your body!
Does this sound weird? Well, you'd better try this. If you pay close attention, you'll realize you have certain cravings. Personally, when I get hungry, when I stop to ask myself that question, I might find I want a chicken salad. Then that's what I for. Your body is always speaking, if you'll listen.

Other times, I might randomly decide to have some snack, but then when I ask myself, "Yo Aron, buddy, are you actually hungry?" I realize there's a huge chance I'm just bored. Then I remember all the stuff I have to do, or stuff I do for leisure, and I go do that instead.

So don't be in a hurry to grab a bite to eat. Listen! And even if you think you really, really want a pizza, slow down and ask yourself, "What else would taste just as good and be twice as healthy?" If you can't figure it out, Google it! Whatever you do, slow down and take your time when it comes to food.

Change The Channel

Eating intelligently means not falling for every stupid advert you see on TV. Companies shell out millions and millions of dollars, year after year, just to get you to buy something. They have experts who are dedicated to figuring out the best way to manipulate your psychology. They want to manipulate you into reaching for your phone and making a call to your favorite burger or pizza joint, and they know ads are effective. Why?

When you're watching TV, your brainwaves are in alpha mode. In this state, you are highly suggestible. So after they've got you in that state of mind with whatever mindless drivel is on, guess what happens next! Ads!

If you have to watch your favorite show, make sure to skip these ads. Change the channel!

These industries do not give a flying fig about you, they just want to make their money, so, they will tell you anything to sell you their product. I think it's very telling their CEOs and executives won't even eat their own products all that often, if at all. What does that tell you? Think!

Trick Yourself

Here's something I did when I was a tad overweight from all that emotional eating, and badly needed to change my life and lose the pounds.

First, I wrote down every single food I knew was my weakness. The pizzas, the burgers, the chocolates, *everything.* A perfect little list of all my little temptations.

Next, beside each item, I wrote out some other healthy food that had the same mouth feel as the unhealthy stuff. Ice cream? No. Yogurt. Chips? No. Homemade, natural popcorn made in a pot, not in the microwave. That sort of thing. Soda? No. Sparkling water.

What did I do after that? I made a commitment to myself I would never use those words - the unhealthy foods - ever again. Not when speaking, and not when thinking. So when I'd start craving a soda, I'd say, "Man, I'm really craving sparkling water." You get it?

After a while, guess what happened? ***I actually started to believe myself!*** I believed I really did want water. I really did want carrots. I really did want fruit.

Another trick I played on myself was saying, "I don't eat THIS." So when I'd see something I liked that was pure junk, I'd remind myself gently, "I DON'T eat this." Not "can't," but DON'T. The distinction is important. It tells my subconscious mind, hey, this is good looking and all but it really isn't my thing. Guess what happens when you program your subconscious with the right messages? It begins to act accordingly!

Things You Can do to Improve Your Health and Cut Down on Emotional Eating

- ### *Water! And more water!*

Feel hungry? First have a glass of water. Still feel hungry? Have another glass. If you're still hungry, then fine, go eat something! Even if you choose junk, you won't have enough room for it.

Staying hydrated is very important for your body's daily function. But many people do not drink enough. About 60 percent of our body is made up of water and that water is used up in transpiration (sweating), transportation of substances etc. And as regularly as it is used up, it also needs to be replaced. For all of you looking for flawless skin without having to buy expensive cosmetic products, water will really help you. It hydrates the skin and helps in the removal of dead skin cells.

Keeping hydrated also helps regulate the body's temperature. So, whenever you feel flushed, just drink a glass of water! It also helps control our blood pressure, and you will be less likely to suffer from a stroke or high blood pressure.

Water aids in the digestion of food and in so doing, helps burn a lot of calories, which research has shown helps a person lose belly fat.

There are a lot of suggestions in the media these days, on how much water a person should consume in a day. But doctors' advice is to stay very hydrated as the health benefits re many and as such have suggested that a person consume at least half a gallon of water in a day.

Don't fret, you don't have to finish it all in one go.

We know how our stomachs seem to slosh from one side to another when we drink too much water. It's not a particularly pleasant feeling. It's actually a real concern for a person not to drink **too much** water. Drinking too much water, too fast, within a short period of time causes our sodium levels to drop too low, which causes water intoxication or hyponatremia.

So you could be "drunk" on water.

- Fruits! And more Fruits!

I am sure we have all heard the old saying, an apple a day keeps the doctor away. It's very true, in the literal sense.

Fruits are naturally low in fat content, carbs and calories but are rich in vitamins. Many fruits are the origin of important nutrients and are not eaten enough. Nutrients such as folic acid, potassium, citric acid and dietary fiber.

Fruits help boost our immune system and gives us a fighting chance against some consuming enough fruits can help reduce our chances of getting heart diseases, elevated blood pressure, even some cancers. *Amazing, right?*

Fruits are vitamin rich foods that help keep our energy levels up. Eating a good amount of fruits is healthy as long as it is part of a healthy diet plan. A fruit-only diet can be dangerous to the health because fruits are rich in natural sugar. If they are over consumed, your blood sugar levels might be elevated to an insanely dangerous height.

If you can squeeze in a small plate of fruit salad after dinner instead of your usual cream filled pastry for dessert, trust me, you will be better for it.

- ***Exercise!* Move it, move it!**

How many times have you watched people engaging in rigorous exercises and you know in your heart of hearts that no matter how much you tried or wanted to, you could never do what they are doing? *I mean, they make it look so simple!*

Their bodies seeming sculpted or honed from pure steel. Beautiful bodies with defined abs. But you are just watching them with your *generous* body. Not fat, *generous.*

You can always remedy that. It doesn't take much. You do not need all those fancy instruments of torture they have at the gym or go under the surgical knife. All you need is your will and a little bit of time.

Try running. It is a cardiovascular exercise. Popularly called "cardio." Why? Because it elevates your heart rate. *Running causes your heart to race!* It is a very healthy exercise that helps build and define muscles. It also helps strengthen our bones, because, during the course of the exercise our bones are made to bear the weight of our body, so they grow stronger so as to be able to withstand the constant pressure they get from being jolted.

Running also helps us stay in the healthy weight range, and helps shed some weight. It also helps our respiration. When we run we burn energy and use up a lot of oxygen. That is why we breathe faster while running. Breathing fast causes us to unconsciously inhale faster, which causes our body to increase the production of oxygen and removal of carbon dioxide.

Many people have also said running helps them think better. And it helps them deal with emotions such as anger, hurt or annoyance. It can even help you feel less lethargic! Fancy that!

When I say running, I don't mean for you to take part in the Olympics, or run 20 miles every day. You could easily run from one end of your street to the other. You don't have to be as fast as Usain Bolt. Go at your own pace. It may be very difficult if you push yourself too hard, especially if it's something you are not particularly used to doing.

Try walking. We all walk, from the car to the house, the local store and back. We may even take a leisurely walk through the park. Walking is just the movement of our legs, one in front of the other in a pattern. You can do that, can't you? Just a 30-minute walk a day can do wonders!

Such a simple physical activity can help burn an impressive amount of calories. If you can dedicate at least forty five minutes of your time to a brisk walk daily, you will begin to noticeably lose weight in no time.

Like running, walking also helps our cardiovascular and pulmonary system. Walking also helps us develop stronger bones and to hone lithe muscles for a better body figure. It reduces our chances of developing a stroke or heart disease, and helps us maintain our blood pressure.

- **Eat All The Green Things! Veggies for the Win!**

And the other stuff.

Vegetables are plants edible to humans. The word is used to classify all parts of an edible plant, including the stem, the root, the flower, the fruit, the seeds and the leaves. There are many different types of vegetables, but the point is to incorporate as many as possible in your meal without being wasteful.

It has been discovered that people who eat enough vegetables and fruits as part of their diet have a reduced risk of having chronic diseases. Vegetables are rich in various nutrients like; vitamins A, E and C, dietary fiber, potassium, and folic acid.

Vegetable diets Help reduce the risk of type-2 diabetes, coronary diseases (heart), stroke, high blood pressure, etc.

- **Go to Sleep!**

We are all well aware of what sleep is. It is something our body needs to be able to function properly. **Sleep** is a state of oneness between the body and the mind which takes place several hours every night, daily. It's a state in which the nervous system is at rest, the eyes are shut and all the muscles in the body are relaxed and our consciousness is temporarily suspended, until our waking moment, where consciousness is regained.

Sleep helps you relieve stress. Maybe after a long day job, after a bout of vigorous exercising, or when you are just bummed out. It also helps reduce depression. Maybe you are feeling depressed over having lost your job, losing a very much needed deal, being broke or watching your favorite team lost the match, a good night's sleep will go a long way. A lot of people have said they tend to feel more alert on waking up. Some even say they tend to remember things they might have forgotten during the day after a good night's rest.

Sleep is a very important part of our lives, there is no way around it. Did you know the less sleep you get, the more likely you are to binge eat when you wake up? So get some good, quality sleep. Don't stare at any screen for an hour before bed. Keep your room nice, dark, and at a cool, comfortable temperature. Invest in good pillows and a solid mattress. It will make all the difference to the quality of your sleep. I promise

If you follow all these tips, what you'll find is that you're going to have more of a handle on your emotional hunger. You'll find your dedication to following these steps will actually spill over, and give you the willpower you need to tell yourself you're not going to have another Twinkie.

Chapter Eight

Dealing With Emotions

First and foremost, what are emotions?

Emotions are a state of the mind related to the nervous system. It is responsible for feelings of pleasure and displeasure, hurt or anger. Emotions are often mistaken for a person's mood, personality, temperament or disposition.

Emotions can be said to be the response or reaction to certain physical or psychological pressures that affect our behavior. They are a very complex concept. Studies show emotions affect a person's cognition. That is why it seems like people who are feeling some kind of strong emotion may not think properly at the time.

Identify Your Emotions

The first step in dealing with one's emotions is identification, figuring out what emotion you are feeling. *Is it pain, anger, hurt or even happiness?* Identifying what you are feeling is a very important step, because it's not so hard for you to deny your emotions, no matter how hard they stare you in the face. This is especially true if you're used to just shoving them aside, rather than processing them in a healthy way.

You could be seething with anger, but just choose to shove it aside, and claim you're fine. Or you could be sad, but you'd rather slap a happy face on, because it's more comfortable for you and everyone. What you're doing is wallowing in denial. When you can't express your emotions, guess what you do as an emotional eater? That's reach! Time to reach for the ol' bag o' chips again. Well, I'm writing this to help you beat that. Once you overcome that, you are ready to deal with your emotions!

It doesn't matter if you are feeling lonely, hurt, stressed, angry, or just plain anxious, it is very important for you to try to find some healthy ways of dealing with these painful emotions. A few emotions are a little less difficult to handle than others. When things start to get really bad, it sometimes feels hard to breathe or cope. Learning to cope with these feelings positively can help you live a healthy and happy life.

Let It Out!

Psychologists have found letting one's emotions out, physically, can go a long way to make that person feel better. If you have a lot of painful emotions bottled inside you, try to punch something - preferably something soft. No, not another human being.

Crying also helps. As does a long, loud scream. You could also jog or run. Or you could try doing what you enjoy, maybe singing, dancing, even playing a video game. Make a freestyle rap about whatever is bothering you. Write it out. Call up a friend and rant. Whatever you need. Just get it all out!

Once emotions are bottled in and suppressed, they become toxic. It is at times like this, when you're feeling emotionally low, that emotional eating is most likely to get the best of you. You know the drill. After you've eaten so much, so fast, you are then riddled by guilt or shame because of that short-lived sweet, sweet indulgence.

Finding A Solution

Once you have identified what you are feeling and have discovered what it means, then you can go ahead and find a solution. Take a moment to ask yourself if there is something you can do to solve the problem, Once your answer is affirmative, what do you do? **Do it!**

For example, if all your attempts at finding a job have proved fruitless, you could have your friends review and rewrite your resume. At that moment, if you feel there is absolutely nothing you can do, try finding out the best way to deal with that feeling of disappointment. Experts have suggested reading, swimming, writing, meditating, getting support from friends and family, exercising and seeking therapy.

Create Your Personal Emotional Toolkit

Consider these methods a toolkit. An emotional tool kit. You simply pick whatever tool it is you might need to deal with your emotions, and then make use of it. Whatever it is you need to use, it had better not be food, or that would completely defeat the purpose! Have you always wanted to learn a new language? Do that! Are you 35 and don't know how to ride a bike? Yay, something to do! Have you been meaning to write some naughty erotica? No time like the present!

Your toolkit could also be a literal toolkit. You should fill the bag with things like your diary, comics, magazines, your favorite music CDs, funny films, your favorite novels, inspirational books. **NO COMFORT FOODS! NO foods, period.**

Different Strokes, Different Folks

Different people have different strategies that work for them. It just depends on your kind of person, how you behave, how you interact with other people, and your ability to deal with your emotions. Your strategy might also vary from day to day! Today, you might want to hit a punching bag to deal with anger. Tomorrow, you might decide to meditate or go for a swim. The next, you might decide to listen to some amazing TED talks.

Mastery of Your Emotions

Emotions often feel overwhelming and intimidating, but taking control of them is usually the best way to deal with them. It may be difficult at first, but once you get the hang of it, it no longer seems so daunting.

Our emotions are like the powerhouse of our beings, as humans. Sometimes it's a good thing. Instead of us being as empty and automated like robots, our emotions push us and motivate us to be better than we are now. The issue is when we let ourselves become prisoners of these emotions. A lot of times, we let temporary emotions or feelings dictate or rule how we make decisions, even when it may lead to regrets in the future

Since most of what we feel and the emotions we go through happen almost instinctively, we have little or no control over how we feel at any given time. But we can try to control how those feelings make us react, by taking the driver's seat on our thoughts.

To be able to interact well, and relate with people, we have to be able to know how people feel too. Because our emotions are the way we speak without actually speaking, without words. There are a lot of ways we can use to tell how other people are feeling, but usually by listening to what they say, and the way they act, most especially their body language.

Experts propose that a little over 80% of human interaction is non-verbal, which means it is usually by body language and facial expression. A lot of people don't like to talk about how they feel if the sense others are going to be affected by what they have to say. So their feelings tend to be more expressed in their body language.

The Limbic System

Emotions are unconscious acts managed by the **limbic system** of the brain. Scientists say this part of the human brain has evolved continuously from early on in human life, which makes it very primitive. This is why our emotional responses are always quite straightforward, but very strong and hard to control. This is because these responses are always controlled by our need to survive.

For a very long time, emotions have been strongly connected to experience and memory. If you have previously suffered a bad experience, your emotional reaction to the same or a similar experience is likely to be just as intense as when you first had the experience.

In that vein, the very first time you were hurt, or something bad (or good!) happened to you, you may have chosen to eat something, just because of how you felt. Now, your brain will have made the connection on your behalf. Anytime something similar to that event happens, you're inclined to do as you did back then. You're inclined to eat! See how this works?

Emotions and Values

Emotions also have a lot to do with a person's values. A person's emotional response can lead you to understand how they feel about something. The way a man might speak about a particular football team can make you understand what his take is on the team. You can even tell if a person likes another person by the way they speak about that person.

Our emotions are the megaphones of our hearts!

Trying to understand this association between our emotions and experience or memory and values gives us the key to controlling our emotional responses. Our emotional responses don't always have to do with whatever we might be going through presently, or what we are thinking about, but by observing your reactions, you may be able to put your emotions in check.

You have to take some time to observe your emotions, the accompanying reactions, and the triggers - be they your values, memories or experiences. Also put into consideration what experiences or values bring about positive emotions, and which ones bring negative ones.

Emotional Distraction Methods

There have been a lot of findings, writings, even suggestions on how to deal with ones emotions. There are a myriad of actions one can take that will be very helpful in dealing with one's emotions. A lot them are very common, but you have to try them to see if they work for you.

Distract yourself.   Yes, it's really necessary. You really, really have to do this. If you are just recovering from a breakup, be proactive about making yourself feel better. Call up a friend and have them tell you all the reasons why you're such a catch! Get a great lineup of comedy shows and movies and prepare to laugh your butt off! Do it just because you deserve some joy in your life. Read a novel, something fascinating or intriguing, or go through a fashion magazine, see what is hot right now, and figure out how you can make it work for you! Learn a new skill from YouTube, or Udemy, or just do whatever will make you happy and keep you distracted! Before you even know it, time has gone by, you have started to feel better. That problem already feels inconsequential.

Exercise whenever you can.   A lot of people have found they have been able to deal with anger or hurt by exercising, whether mildly or vigorously. Some have said they even go as far as imagining the face of the person who hurt or provoked them, while hitting a punching bag. It may seem a bit crude or violent but it helps! Exercise releases "feel good" chemicals in the brain such as **dopamine**, *the dope chemical*, which makes you feel better. Pretty dope, right? Being fit also makes look and feel healthier, which helps in dealing with one's emotions. It's *either this or indulging in comfort foods. I am sure we now understand that emotional eating can be very bad!*

Be thankful for the little things. Appreciate people when they do nice things for you, preferably in person, and try not to forget it. Be thankful for the clothes you have, the roof over your head, the fact that you're not starving. Be thankful for the weather, rain or shine. Be thankful for all sorts of things, and people!

Have fun! Having fun means doing things you enjoy. Do things that make you happy. Do things that are good for you and have no adverse effect on your health. Just have fun! The more you seek it out, the more it will seek **you** out!

Build relationships with others. Interacting with others stops you from always worrying about yourself. Open up to people, make friends, trust a little. Try to be grateful for the little moments of goodness and avoid unnecessary criticism others and yourself, no matter the situation. Always be mindful of your surroundings, and watch what you say to others. Don't you purposely hurt another person's feelings, because in the long run it may come back to bite you in the ass. Talk to someone. It feels good to talk to someone who listens. Spend time with people, doing things that make you both happy. You will be better off for it. You even feel happier because it will take your mind of some personal issues.

Don't give in to negative thinking. If you find you ever find yourself drowning in negative thoughts, then push yourself to overcome them, swim to the surface, get some much needed air and swim to shore. Never let yourself be pulled back in. Go for a walk outside. Inhale deeply and breathe in some fresh air, close your eyes and feel yourself breaking out from whatever negative contraction is around you. Take beautiful Mother Nature in. Notice the greens of the leaves, the chirping of the birds.

Realize deeply and fully that you are not alone. It is very helpful in calming whatever raging emotions you might be feeling.

Psychologists have observed that a change of scenery goes a very long way in recovery. Go camping or hiking and clear your mind. *Just have some fun! It's that simple!* If you do not have the money to go hiking or camping or maybe go on a road trip, you could always go to places you know you will meet people you have never met before. You could go to the market, not necessarily to shop, but to be among new faces to distract yourself. You could go window shopping in the mall. Look for that beautiful shoe that you would love to get if you get enough money, then work out how to get the money to buy that beautiful shoe. It will give your mind something else to bother about.

Appreciate the good things in your life.

Simply put, count your blessings! Yes, I've already talked about this, but it bears repeating! Someday soon, I will write a book about the sheer power of appreciation. It's amazing, and you **will** begin to see changes in your life once you learn to truly appreciate. Trust me on that.

If you can manage to balance your emotions, without hurting any other person's feelings in the process, then you have successfully learnt how to deal with your emotions.

Chapter Nine

Finding the Right Food Balance

I am sure at some point or the other in our lives we have heard about **balanced diets**. We might even have been thought about it in school, if we still remember clearly.

Balanced Diets

A balanced diet is a diet with foods which have enough of the right nutrients in them to nourish your body, so it functions as it needs to.

To get the best from your daily diet, it is advisable that you consume the majority of your daily calories in:

- Fruits
- Leafy greens (vegetables)
- Grains and nuts
- Proteins
- Legumes

Calories

The amount of calories in a meal is measured by the amount of energy stored in that food. Your body needs the calories from your food to fulfill your body's needs and carry out your daily activities such as walking, thinking, breathing, and many other important daily functions.

The average person needs to consume about 2,000 calories daily to maintain a normal body weight. However, daily calorie intake varies from person to person, depending on the person's age, sex, and how active the person is. Men normally burn more calories than women, and active people generally need more calories than people who aren't active.

Where you get your calories from is just as important as the amount of calories you consume. You should try to reduce the amount of empty calories you consume; empty calories are those that have little or no nutritional value. Empty calories are consumed daily in foods such as cakes, cookies, bacon, sausage, cheese, soda, pizza, and energy drinks.

This is why having a balanced diet is so important.

A balanced diet is essential to the proper function of our organs and tissues. They need proper nourishment to work effectively. Without good nutrition, our body is more susceptible to disease and infection, fatigue, and low performance. Children with poor diets are prone to maldevelopment and stunted growth, poor performance educationally, and poor and unhealthy eating habits or patterns that can go on for the rest of their lives.

The ever increasing levels of obesity and diabetes in America are perfect examples of the effects of poor diet and a lack of exercise. These are the leading causes of coronary diseases, cancer, diabetes, and stroke, to name a few.

At the heart of all balanced diets, there are foods with low fats and sugars, which have a high mineral content, vitamins, and other nutrients. Here is a list of food groups that are an essential part of a balanced diet.

www.bigstock.com · 235214953

Fruits

Besides being really tasty and juicy, fruits are a good source of much needed nutrients. Whenever you feel like eating fruits, always get the ones that are in season at the time. They are usually fresher and provide the most nutrients.

Fruits have very high sugar content. These kind of sugars are called "**natural sugars**" because, they are not manmade or processed. So fruits can be a better choice if you are craving something sweet without having to go for processed products. If you are trying to monitor your sugar intake or if you have diabetes, you may want to go for fruits that are low in sugar. People who are trying to monitor their intake of "carbs" might want to go for fruits like melons and avocados.

Vegetables

Vegetables or veggies as most call them, are a primary source of vitamins and minerals. Dark, leafy greens usually contain the most nutrients and can be eaten anytime. One can have a variety of vegetables at every meal, it is very healthy.

Examples of very healthy dark, leafy greens include broccoli, green beans, Swiss chard, spinach, collard greens, and kale. This is by no means an exhaustive list.

Grains

A lot of people consume refined white flour more than any other grain in the world. It's in our cakes, our doughnuts, our pizzas, our buns, our everything. Refined white flour isn't as nutritional as it should be, because the hull of the grain, or outer shell, is usually removed during the refining process. The hull is the most nutritious part of the grain, and it all gets thrown away.

Whole grains, however, are prepared using the entire grain, including the hull. They are more nutritious that way. You should try eating more whole grain products instead of white flour products.

Proteins

Meats and beans are our main sources of protein. A protein is a nutrient; an amino acid that plays an important role in proper muscle development, and brain function and development. Lean, white meats that are low in fat, such as chicken, fish, and certain parts of pork and beef are the best. Cutting away the skin and trimming off solid fat on the meats are easy ways to reduce the amount of fat and cholesterol. Grass-fed animals are the ideal choice in meat because the health and fatty acid content of meat is affected by the animal's nutrition

Beans and some nuts are very good sources of protein too, and have many health benefits and can contain dietary fiber too. Try to eat lentils, walnuts, peas, sunflower seeds, almonds, and beans. Tofu, tempeh, and other soy-based products are very protein rich and are a healthy alternative for vegetarians.

Dairy

Dairy products are products filled with milk or made from milk. They are rich in calcium, vitamin D, and other important nutrients. However, they're also one of the major sources of fat, so it would be wiser to choose full-fat cheeses in small amounts, and reduce your yogurt intake. Plant-based milk, such as those made from soy, coconut, almonds, or rice are typically rich in calcium and many other nutrients, making them good and safer substitutes to dairy from cows.

Oils

Oils should be consumed as little as possible. It is more advisable to go for low-fat and low-sugar versions of oily products, such as mayonnaise and salad dressings. Healthy oils, such as olive oil, can be used to replace fattier vegetable oil our diets. Most importantly, try to avoid deep-fried foods like fries, because they contain many empty calories.

While maintaining a balanced diet, there are a lot of substances to avoid which are harmful and/or contain no nutritional value. I'm talking about stuff like excess salts, saturated fats, sugars, alcohol, refined grains, trans fats, and solid fats.

If you are not sure of your dietary habits or you feel you are doing something wrong, you can always schedule an appointment with a dietician. They we help you revise your eating plan and come up with a better one and help you maintain a balanced diet.

Chapter Ten

Say No to Food Addiction

As I've already said, when emotional eating gets out of hand, it can easily lead to food addiction. At this point you can't just help yourself. You look forward to your next "fix." Even when you are at work and it's not long after your lunch break, and you already had lunch fit for a Sumo wrestler, you start to get "the itch."

You may be wondering how possible it is to get "high" on food. Well, I already explained all that in the previous chapters. It's possible thanks to a hormone called dopamine, which gives you that rush when you eat. Ever moan or sigh when you eat something that tastes so good? That's that dopamine rush, coursing through you.

The Problem of Food Addiction

See it's not just about eating way too much at mealtimes. Food addiction involves eating more than you need, even when you're not hungry! This is where the problem lies. Say you've been able to identify you have a problem, and you've tried to quit. Then you fail. Don't beat up on yourself! The reason is you start to have withdrawal symptoms, since you're addicted. And since food is such a normal thing to have - unlike hard drugs - no one's going to try to stop you. Heck, you'll even find yourself justifying it. You've been good! You haven't eaten anything for like, three whole minutes! You've earned this pizza!

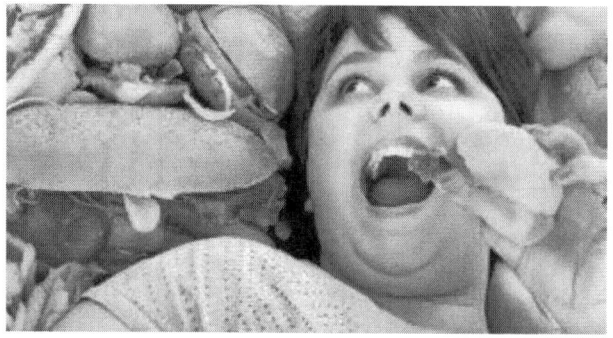

Food addiction arises when we eat for pleasure, rather than for sustenance. People who have that "sweet tooth" can relate a little too well to eating for pleasure. I'm one of said people. I will not deny it. It's just that I have over the years learned how to handle myself and my love for the sweet stuff.

When you reach for the sweets, you do so out of a craving for that rush of dopamine. You do it over and over and over, and not unlike with drug use, you start to need more sweets than in the beginning to feel the same high. Your body has come to expect it, and so you've simply got to deliver, or else it's going to throw a hissy fit by making you feel crappy.

So if you always end the day with a slice of chocolate cake, for instance, your body comes to expect that. It's become a habit. A routine. What happens when you don't give yourself that slice? Your body gets mad! But you don't even have to worry about that, because you've become so used to having a slice that you will find yourself unconsciously getting a slice even after committing to not doing that!

I have had people tell me sometimes, no other place will do except so-and-so store. They want their sweet treat from a particular place or store. All other chocolate cakes seem inferior, or just don't quite hit the spot right.

If you're this person, chances are you're addicted. When you decide to withdraw from the food, you get a reaction. Sometimes you get flu-like symptoms.

There will be headaches, stomach upsets, and pure fatigue. Sometimes, you might not even realize that's what's going on. That's why a lot of people tend to feel like crap once they haven't had their morning shot of coffee. About 90 percent of Americans consume at least one cup of coffee a day, and 70 percent of these people can't start their day without one. A lot of people say they feel more alert and reinvigorated after a cup of Joe, and when they don't drink it the whole day seems to be difficult somehow. Many of them do not realize they are addicted!

Sometimes, you can get these withdrawal symptoms when you switch diets. Why is this key? You need to know so you don't quit when the symptoms come in.

Food Withdrawal

You see, it will take you about 2 weeks from when you start eating right to feel better. In the beginning of your new, improved, healthy way of eating, you'll feel like crap. You'll feel like you're currently unable to do it. And that's okay. Just wait it out. Trust the process. In a couple of weeks, you'll find yourself feeling better than you've felt in years. That's a guarantee. Reports show symptoms start to reduce after the first week, but you might feel very tired and drained for the first two weeks, or three if your addiction is *that* severe.

People do not understand the seriousness of food addiction because they can't seem to wrap their minds around how withdrawal from a simple thing like sugar should be associated with withdrawal from hard drugs like cocaine.

An addiction is an addiction. Your food addiction might not be as severe as withdrawing from drugs, but it is what it is. A positive change to your diet is very important regardless of the withdrawal symptoms you might have, because you will feel better for it.

It's NOT The Healthy Food Causing Your Symptoms!

A lot of people who have noticed they are having withdrawal symptoms think it is because of the foods or diets they are withdrawing from, when in reality it is the food changes to are making that cause the symptoms of withdrawal.

You can't just go from a mixed diet to an all-meat or all-greens plan; your body will show signs of confusion first, before you adapt.
Psychologists say experiments have shown food rich in carbs and processed sugar affect the brain the same way hard drugs like cocaine do, and so, suffering a modicum of withdrawal symptoms is perfectly normal.

This is the reason why people experience things like "sugar rush" because at that moment your brain lights up and your dopamine receptors go into overdrive, so you become alert and hyperactive. Doctors have found that sugar targets a person's basic pleasure and reward circuitry, this is what brings on the sugar rush, resulting in something akin to food addiction.

The amazing thing is symptoms of food withdrawal don't last long compared to withdrawal symptoms from hard drugs, which is a difficult and harrowing can even hasten the process of withdrawal by staying hydrated, eating olives and avocados process. You and drinking plant based milk like almond, soy, rice, etc.

There is still a lot of speculation on whether food addiction and withdrawal is "real," so, it would be wise not to take any drastic measures to deal with food addictions and emotional eating, because you might just be doing more harm than good. Here is a list of things expert dieticians and psychologists suggest when you feel you have a food addiction you are trying to withdraw from.

- **Tread carefully**

You need to be cautious and mindful of your withdrawal approach. If you rush headfirst into it, you might end up hurting yourself. It won't do for you to jump from one problem to another. It would be very unwise to cut off entire food groups at a go, especially macronutrients like carbohydrates, proteins, and fats. After all, the aim is having a balanced diet. Any slight mistake might plunge you head long into food imbalance. Results are better when withdrawal is done gradually, with a few indulgences here and there. Maybe a glass of wine on a special day, pizza with friends on a good weekend and so on.

- **Seek help from a professional**

Withdrawing from food addiction is not the same as withdrawing from alcohol or drug addiction, and does not even pose the same health risks. Still, it would be wise to seek professional help. It is important to talk to a dietitian or doctor about what you are planning to do so that you can share your concerns with them, and if they have any problems with your plan, they can put you through the proper way. They might recommend dietary supplements to make up for the reduced nutrients in your new course of action.

- **Do not rush things**

Some people expect a change in diet to make them feel better instantly. That is not usually the case. One has to first feel worse before getting better. It's the way of things. You know, "It's always darkest before the dawn." So instead of an abrupt cut, you could try steadily reducing the amount of calories you are trying to cut back on until you are left with very little or nothing.

A lot of people have noticed that after three weeks or more of steady withdrawal, they are almost unable to stomach the foods they used to abuse. Sugary confections taste even sweeter than they used to taste, while some foods can go as far as making you nauseated, especially really oily foods.

- **Try a calculated approach**

If you are withdrawing from sugary foods, you might have a really hard time of it. All your senses will willingly betray you. You feel like you smell chocolate everywhere. You could swear that book on your table looked like a piece of chocolate five minutes ago.

It's just a brown colored book!

It may seem like you are going crazy, but it won't last. You are just weaning yourself off of the sugar. If you know you will surely give in to temptation, then strategize, come up with different plans, and cross them out as you go until you find what works for you.

Planning ahead is very important. Clear your home and office of every tempting morsel of chocolate, make sure not to pass in front of the store where you usually buy your stash from. Include your friends and family in your strategy so they can help build your fortitude. It will be good for them too. If you find yourself in a place where everybody for some reason or the other is eating chocolate, run for your dear life!

Retreat! Retreat!

There is no shame in cowardice in this scenario. Be a healthy coward who has a low risk of having diabetes.

You could always find healthier food choices. I once suggested to a friend to cook something healthy and give it a chocolatey name. It might just work for you too. *Why not try spinach sauce au chocolàt!* Mind you, no real chocolates should be used. This is just a way of consoling yourself and getting your mind off things.

Coming up with a name could be very fun too!

Also try to surround yourself with people who are like minded or have the same plans that you do. It's a great way to make friends, and you all can find something to laugh about! Trust me, the whole experience can be very funny when you have people with a sense of humor to share it with.

Learn to Cook

It is important to learn how to cook. If you already do, good for you! if you don't, then invest in a recipe book. Because the reason a lot of withdrawals from food addiction don't work is that people that don't know how to cook, or are too lazy to cook, so they tend to fall back into take-out habits. And most of the choices they tend to make are usually unhealthy.

While withdrawing from food addiction, try to have fun creating healthier options for yourself. It makes the process a lot easier and takes your mind off of things, and before you know it, it's all over. Your food addiction a thing of the past.

Chapter Eleven

Satisfaction, Not Deprivation

Before we can go further, we have to be able to understand what **satisfaction** and **deprivation** mean.

First of all, satisfaction is the feeling of contentment one gets when they have done or gotten they wanted for some time. People mostly feel satisfied once they have fed their emotional hunger, even though that satisfaction doesn't last. A person is said to be satisfied when their emotions are over washed by a feeling of fulfillment or contentment.

Deprivation, on the other hand, means withholding something from one's self even when it is absolutely necessary. Some say it's an act of self-punishment, especially in the throes of shame and guilt. A person might starve themselves just because they indulged a little too much when they knew they shouldn't have.

Whenever you do something for yourself, something you feel is right for you, something that makes you happy and gives you joy, there is always an accompanying feeling of self-satisfaction. Basically, your mind is telling you that it is pleased with you.

Deprivation mostly accompanies the feeling of satisfaction in emotional eaters. Many of them feel ashamed that they are enjoying anything at all when they do not look good enough, or fit enough. Some seek to deprive themselves after straying from their diet, as if to make up for the little blunder.

It doesn't have to always be that way. You have to feel good about yourself. It's your right, and no one can take it away from you.

Satisfaction is our brain's emotional reward system. That feeling is always there to let you know when you are doing the right things. I should probably point out that feeling satisfied doesn't necessarily mean you have done the right thing. Eating that plate of pasta must have left you feeling satisfied, even when it sabotaged your dietary plans.

Satisfaction is an emotion that is very easy to identify.

When you are going on a diet plan, always aim to arrange it in such a way it doesn't feel like a chore or a trip to the doctor's office. Aim to please yourself, because at the end of the day, it's only your opinion that matters.

Depriving yourself of certain things is also not a solution. In some cases, it can be bad for our health. For example, depriving yourself of food because you over indulged is really not a good idea. Your body needs nutrients to function. What you should do instead is give it more of the right stuff, and less of the bad stuff.

If you care so much about other people's opinions, hear me now: your actions don't affect them. They affect **you**. So, be careful when you feel you need to deprive yourself to fit some ridiculous standard you perceive everyone around you has set for you. Deprivation only ever makes things worse! Not better. I mean, why would you deprive yourself of food when your body needs those nutrients to survive? Without the food, you'd die!

I'm not talking about fasting here. That's different, and deliberate, and borne out of a sheer desire to reset the system. If that's what you're doing then great! Just be sure to follow medical advice while you're at it. But if this is a guilt thing, then you're depriving yourself, and I promise it's a circle that never ends. You're only going to binge again. Your brief moment of satisfaction shouldn't end in endless hours of agony just because you made a mistake. Move on!

Don't Beat Yourself Up

I know there have been a lot of instances where you browbeat yourself before or after you eat something.

At that moment, your thoughts are everywhere, and you start to wonder if you really should have eaten what you ate. You wonder what would happen if you eat a certain food. You wonder how to make up for enjoying that juicy burger a little too much. *Need I continue?*

That voice inside your head that brow beats you at every given opportunity is an enemy. An enemy you need to vanquish. This enemy is rooted so deep in your mind it never even occurs to you to question it. You decide to order in a box of pizza after a long day at work and that voice in your head starts to scream and rant after you've had the pizza already. "Pizzas are terrible! They will make you fat! You will never lose weight at this rate! You should have eaten a bowl of fruit salad instead! Now we're going to have to fix this! What do we do? No food for the next five months!"

Do Away with Labels

Yes, we know certain foods really are good or bad for you. But! We need to help you actually be able to do away with guilt. See, once you stop feeling guilty for eating something, you're better able to make better decisions and choices for your body. So how do we achieve this?

Don't label your food. I t may seem counterintuitive, but don't. At best, just tell yourself, "I eat this, I don't eat that." Don't be forceful about it. Just gently tell yourself that when dealing with temptations. .

You see, putting good or bad labels on foods stops you from actually enjoying what you are eating, whether or not it really is good or bad! Once you have already decided a food is bad, you will be engulfed by a feeling of guilt and shame which in most cases leads you to deprive yourself of something else you like as punishment. You'll become so obsessed with what to eat or not eat that all that analysis paralysis will just leave your brain fried. Remember what you do when you're overwhelmed? **You go for the easiest option.** And that just keeps you stuck in emotional eating mode.

Emotional eating usually makes this even worse and feelings of guilt or shame easily result in self-derision, self-loathing, self-deceiving, ruin, hopelessness, and shame. To rid yourself of that feeling of having lost all control of yourself, you start to feel like you have to make up for it using self-destructive behaviors and self-imposed rules. You start to feel bad and worthless if you wolf down a snack just before dinner. You feel bad for eating when you feel like you should be exercising. After all, that's what others are doing.

You are not them!

These feelings of guilt and self-deprivation are always as a result of fear of failure. This fear may push you to punish yourself with destructive behaviors like drug abuse, smoking, alcohol abuse, compulsive exercising and so on.

Never Enough

What people do not know is that these feelings aren't necessarily related to food. They are just as a result of one's inability to accept and love yourself unconditionally, because that nagging and annoying voice in your head keeps telling you that you are not good enough, pretty enough, smart enough or funny enough.

These feelings of guilt or shame after eating something "bad" or doing something you feel you shouldn't have is just your way of dealing with the feeling. If you start to feel bad about everything that enters your mouth, before long, what you eat will be what defines your mood.

Man, Know Thyself

Observing your behavioral pattern is an important part of your recovery. The rules, the "good" and "bad" labels, the deprivation and self-destructive derision stop you from seeking any form of help. This is because you have become your own judge and jury system. Sorting out the jungle that is your feelings, learning how to enjoy food again is one of the surest ways to recovery.

More often than not, we eat based on our feelings, and a lot of times, food affects the way we feel. Eating goes way beyond physical hunger, even though, granted, we eat when we are hungry. We eat to fill out bellies. We eat to be satisfied; to have feelings of pleasure and fulfillment. We have to understand the reasoning behind our food choices to be able to feel satisfied with our choice.

How to Be Satisfied With Your Food

With such a wide range of foods to choose from, how does one get satisfaction from food? Most importantly, feelings of satisfaction differ from person to person. While a person might derive pleasure and satisfaction from eating a home-cooked meal in a cost environment, another might enjoy eating a bit of chocolate while working.

Consuming food is a repetitive action. It's one our survival depends on. A person may crave something sugary, but still won't get that satisfaction from eating a very succulent apple. One might want to go for something even more sugary than that. So, a piece of chocolate would seem a better option to that person, as opposed to the apple, just to fill that void or hole they may feel in their emotions. Although a person might feel some satisfaction from doing this, feelings of shame or guilt follow closely behind.

Eating to cope can increase negative responses and emotions towards food, especially in the end. The cause of the stress is temporarily forgotten because we are more focused on our fat, oil, and sugar-filled food choices. Regular consumption of unhealthful foods can result in unnecessary weight gain, poor self-esteem, and bad body image. When we have negative feelings about ourselves, it speeds up the process of guilt and shame, and accelerates the movement of the cycle.

Attaining Maximum Satisfaction

If we are trying to get the ultimate satisfaction, we have to eradicate every feeling of guilt, shame, self-derision, deprivation, and self-loathing following each meal. Although food should not be used as a reward system all the time, a glass of wine during Thanksgiving or eating a slice of cake on your birthday is perfectly acceptable.

So, no need to be mad at yourself!

If you know you will always be racked with guilt whenever you eat something, try to find something you can eat without being filled with shame. Some people can eat nuts without being filled with guilt. They are perfectly healthy. Having a healthy relationship with the foods you eat is very important as it keeps us in touch with our external and internal environment. It helps us deal with our muddled emotions and find a way to reduce disordered patterns and thoughts.

The purpose of that small voice in our head is to whisper needed suggestions that can help us make better choices, but it can be a bit warped, twisted into a little monster of criticism from our guilt. We have to always bear it at the back of our minds eating that bit of chocolate fudge at the end of a stressful day will not make the day any less stressful than it actually was. It won't even give your body the essential nutrients that it needs. *So why bother?*

You have to be able to understand your body's language, and be cognizant of any signal your body gives, especially it's yelling at you, "Hey, buddy, I am full!" Understanding these signals help us make better choices towards better health and general wellness, as opposed to guilt and deprivation.

Chapter Twelve

The Repercussions of Emotional Eating

We have already ascertained emotional eating can have very dangerous consequences to our physical health, mental health, even our social life.

One study was carried out which proved that there is no such thing as a "comfort food."

What?

With your level of intelligence and intellectual ability, you must have already noticed that the so called "comfort foods" we have around provides little comfort.

Comfort Foods Are Not Real

An experiment was carried out on a group of self-acclaimed chocolate lovers. The researchers induced stress in the participants by having them all insert their hands in cold water for some time. It's probably not you would call stress... after all, it is not as back-breaking as the stress you get from work challenges and all, but the body reacts the same way to all types of stress.

Anyway, the participants were then given hand grips so the researchers could measure how much effort they put into gripping them in order to get a piece of chocolate. It may sound a little bit silly to you, but the results were anything but.

Stress As A Motivator

The truth is stress makes us crave rewards and pushes us to get them. How many times have you found yourself motivating yourself to finish that last bout of vigorous exercise so you could get yourself a good cold glass of water? Or have you ever promised yourself a big piece of chocolate if you were able to finish a task you set for yourself? Then you can relate to what I'm saying.

This research also shows we do not always derive the amount of pleasure from the reward as we expect. This study was conducted at the University of Geneva, Switzerland. So you know they must have used only the best quality chocolate.

When we are stressed, cortisol, one of the many hormones I mentioned in one of the previous chapters, surges forward, making us start to crave things we know we shouldn't, things we wouldn't even think of on a normal day. No matter how tempting it may seem, emotional eating doesn't really deal with stress the way we'd like it to. It just postpones it for another time. SO rather than grab a bar of chocolate, lace up your shoes and go for a jog! Work up a proper sweat!

Working out is a great way to relieve yourself of stress. By the time you're all done, nice and sweaty, you're going to find you've completely forgotten you had a craving to begin with.

Effects of Emotional Eating

Emotional eating has become one of a very long list of problems which not only mess up our psyche, but wreaks havoc on our physical health, too. People have been known to eat for many different reasons besides hunger.

Emotional eating can stem from many issues. Some people have even claimed to develop the habit as a side effect of some medicines such as birth control.

There are a lot of side effects to emotional eating, both physical and emotional. We shall see a few of them before we look into healthier methods of feeding. I know you already know a few of these detrimental repercussions of giving in to emotional hunger, but let's just go over some of the major ones really quick.

- **Feeling shame or guilt**   After whatever emotional crisis we are going through, we are usually flooded by a huge wave of shame or guilt, especially when we realize how much we have chowed in our bid to deal with this emotional crisis. This feeling of shame also has the ability to further plunge us in a gaping emotional hole, causing us to eat again, and again, and again, and that vicious cycle continues.

- **Bouts of nausea**   A lot of people who suffer from panic attacks or anxiety attacks are usually comforted by the "feelings" they have in their stomach which they mistaken as need for food. This often results in bouts of nausea after they have over indulged. These bouts of nausea are sometimes quite severe, and sometimes these symptoms may persist even after days of having indulged. This usually puts them off other foods for some time until the process is repeated again.

- **Health complications** There are a lot of health problems related to repetitive indulgence in emotional eating. Health conditions like type 2 diabetes, elevated blood pressure, extreme fatigue. and obesity are all examples of how our bodies bear the brunt of our overindulgence.

- **Lack of focus** People often see food as a method of distracting them from their problems. A most effective way of dealing with emotional eating is finding another distraction. Some people start to feel lost, or they lose focus when they do not have food to soothe them. It is a bad habit, and if left unchecked, it can leave a person regularly distracted. If you always find yourself reaching for food to distract yourself, then find something else to distract you. Try distractions that have definite health benefits such as bicycling or going for a walk in the park, or even going out with a couple of friends. While it may seem the main problem is you have no control over what you eat, emotional eating actually starts with our lack of control over our emotions.

- **Excessive weight gain** This is one of the first noticeable side effects of emotional eating.

Excessive weight puts a lot of pressure on our bones and muscles. You start to feel muscle and joint pain. You also feel tired, irritated, and in extreme cases, you may not be to bear your body's weight.

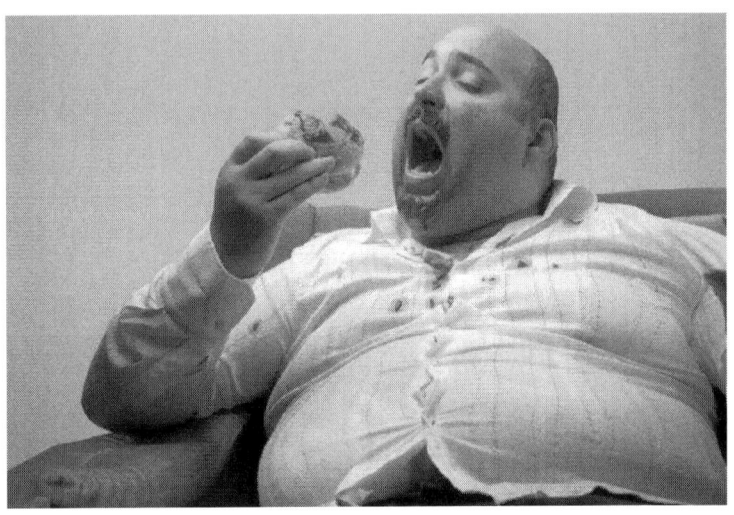

- **Lack of confidence and self-esteem**
  People have undergone excessive weight gain tend to worry a lot about physical appearances and social acceptance. This causes a steady decline in their self-esteem and confidence. They tend to deprive themselves of the food they feel make them fat and in turn tend to eat more from hunger

- **Emotional distress**

  When a person ends up realizing the consequences of their overindulgence, it's usually too late. This further depresses them and causes undue distress. You start to have feelings of paranoia and start to see snide looks where there are none. In the long run, you still continue to overeat as a way to soothe your distress. When you eventually get depressed, you eat more and more to counter the effect of these negative emotions

- **Increased metabolic imbalance**

  After some time, you start to have metabolic imbalances due to fluctuations in electrolyte levels which result in increased levels of anxiety, loneliness, and frustration. At this point you find it difficult to perform simple tasks. The sight of food makes you more and more insecure about yourself.

- **Affects your relationships**   Emotional eating affects our relationship with family, relatives, and friends. This is usually because food and the need for the next "fix" becomes your major concern, so you have no time for any other thing. After all, that burger has to come out of your mouth before you can talk to anybody!

- **Digestive problems** Once your diet starts to consist only of high fat junk food and high calorie foods, you open yourself to different kinds of gastrointestinal problems which can cause serious damage to your digestive system. You become very prone to different kinds of allergic reactions because your body can no longer deal with the large quantities of junk you now consume very regularly. Your system might not be able to cope if you persist with such a really bad diet.

- **High cholesterol levels** Emotional eating makes you very susceptible to diseases that are caused by high cholesterol and high blood sugar levels due to excessive consumption of food.

- **Organ Malfunction**   Another health risk of emotional eating excesses is organ malfunction. Your liver, kidney, stomach, and other organs in the body which handle digestion and nutrient assimilation then become extremely prone to diseases and disorders.

- **Skin related problems**   When we consume too much high fat junk foods, we increase the oil levels in our body, which can lead to many skin-related problems like acne and pimples.

- **Acid reflux**   Excessive emotional eating can increase acidity levels in our bodies which causes a serious digestive condition called acid reflux.

- **Poor oral hygiene**   People who overeat focus so much on putting food in their mouth that they rarely have the time to brush and clean their teeth properly. I don't have to tell you the sort of havoc that wreaks on their dental health. And since oral hygiene has been linked to a lot of serious diseases, then that just makes things worse for the emotional overeater.

- **Drowsiness**   Emotional eaters are mostly so caught up in food that sometimes they lose their train of thought and focus. Most times they are found dozing off at the place where they just, sometimes with their hands still in the pack of chips.

If you want to avoid all of this, then you had better implement the plans and tips I've given you in this book so far! No time like the present to get started.

Chapter Thirteen

The Benefits of Physical Activity

Physical activity simply means expending energy through the movement of one's body. Walking, dancing, waving, climbing the stairs, skating, playing soccer, or bending over to pick a fallen item are all good examples of physical activities. Physical activities can be either moderate or vigorous.

Is Physical Activity Exercise?

The word "exercise" should never be used to replace the term "physical activity," because exercise is a subdivision of physical activity that is usually planned out, structured, repeated, and purposeful. This means exercise is about the enhancement of physical fitness. Being fit is the main objective behind a structured physical activity as exercise. All exercises is physical activity, but not all physical activity counts as exercise. Lifting food to your mouth is a physical activity. It most definitely is **not** exercise.

Besides exercise, physical activity involves skeleto-muscular movements. If you're doing chores at home, playing sports, working, or moving your body one way or another, that's obviously physical activity.

Physical activity or exercise has a lot of health benefits and reduces your risk of developing different diseases like type 2 diabetes, some cancers and heart disease. Physical activity and exercise usually have both long-term and short-term benefits. Most importantly, routine physical exercising improves your way of life. At least thirty minutes of physical activity daily is enough to put you in premium health.

Physiological Benefits of Physical Activity and Exercise

If you stay physically active as much as possible, you will:

- Reduce your risk of getting a heart attack by at least 30%
- Manage and maintain your weight easily
- Reduce your blood cholesterol level
- Reduce your risk of getting type 2 diabetes and some cancers

- Maintain your blood pressure
- Have stronger bones, well defined muscles and joints and reduce your risk of developing osteoporosis
- Be less prone to fall
- Be able to recover quickly from any bouts of illness that you might have
- Be able to sleep and relax better

Psychological Benefits of Physical Activity and Exercise

Studies have shown that exercise helps depression. Many conclusions have been drawn on how exactly exercise helps depression:

- Exercise can serve as a distraction from your overwhelming emotions.
- Exercising creates an opportunity for social interaction. You could make new friends at the gym and they can help you in your weight loss program.

- Exercise releases "feel good" hormones, so it makes it easier for you to let loose and relax or even sleep.
- Exercise is a great stress-relief method

Being physically active is a lot better than doing nothing at all. Not only is good for your physical health, it improves your mental health too. If you have never been one to engage in physical activities, start by going slow until you can steadily progress into the recommended amount.

Try to be as active as possible every day. Add up at least 2-5 hours of moderate physical activity or 1-3 hours of vigorous physical activity, or an equal combination of both every week. Try to do muscle defining exercises at least two days a week.

Steady increase in our physical activity such as skating, walking or cycling instead of driving, using the train or even using the bus is good for us. This is how you get fit and **stay fit**, regardless of age or gender.

I have mentioned before how low physical activity increases your risk of coronary diseases, stroke, diabetes, osteoporosis, and possibly an early death. I am sure after reading of the consequences associated with lack of physical activity, you just might be among the third of the world's population who have resolved to exercise more.

Physical Activity and Mental Health

Rates of anxiety and depression are at their highest recorded levels in Asia, Europe and North America. Undoubtedly, many aspects of our daily life contribute to this problem. However, inactivity is one of the key reasons.

Most of us have experienced how a short walk in the park or little time at the gym improves our moods for a while. Exercise is very well known for stimulating the brain to produce "feel good" hormones. These hormones usually help us deal with strong emotions or problems. They make our issues feel more manageable.

Focusing on exercise can help us deal with what's important. Depending on the kind of exercise, a person might feel energized, relaxed or may even want to interact with other people. All of this goes a long way towards improving our mental health and helping us handle our emotions better.

Download from
Dreamstime.com
The watermarked comp image is for previewing purposes only

84197467
Wanda Orea | Dreamstime.com

However, many people do not know how important physical activity is to mental health because there has been a wide separation in the definition of "body" and "mind."

In fact, Increasingly more accurate research has proven physical activity not only maintains our mental health, but it can also be used to treat some chronic diseases. Now, we know the likelihood of depression and some mental diseases reduce with increased physical activity. Clinically, exercise has been known to work as well as medicines in some kind of mental conditions such as mild to moderate depression, anxiety, and it even reduces cognitive problems in schizophrenia.

How does exercise do all this?

Simply put, exercise has a direct effect on the human brain. Regular exercise creates better blood flow to some parts of the brain, which increase in volume due to the increased flow of blood to such regions and also helps maintain neuronal health due to the increased transport of nutrients and oxygen to the brain, and through an increase of neurohormones that help our central nervous system function properly.

The part of the brain that is of great importance to mental health is the **hippocampus**, an area of the brain involved in cognition, emotion, memory, and learning. Experts have discovered increased physical activity helps in the creation of new neurons in the hippocampus. This process is known as neurogenesis.

These experts have also found evidence which proves many mental illnesses are a result of poor neurogenesis in the hippocampus. This has been considered to be more severe in depression. Surprisingly enough, many antidepressants once thought to reduce or stop depression by the effect of the drugs on serotonin levels, have now been shown to increase neurogenesis in the hippocampus of the patient.

You may wonder what this all means.

Well, scientists say newborn hippocampal neurons are better at keeping new memories, and making old and new memories separate and unique. So, neurogenesis helps us develop our cognitive abilities and sharpen our mental reflexes.

Many mental illnesses are known for impairing cognitive flexibility. And when we have little or no cognitive flexibility, it makes us repeat unhealthy behaviors. It impairs our ability to acknowledge new information and process old ones, and reduces our problem solving abilities. Therefore, it is safe to conclude physical activity helps improve mental health by increasing cognitive flexibility.

If a person adheres to 40-60 minutes of exercise for at least three days a week, it can help them deal with even chronic depression. The effects start to show after a month or so of a religious routine, which incidentally is how long it takes for neurogenesis to be completed. Continuous training should continue for at least twelve weeks more until all signs of depression are gone.

With these modern magic weight loss and fitness schemes, this may seem a little too much, but no genuine mental health solution comes easy. Exercising moderately and at your own pace still works and of course the result of this continued activity are pretty awesome!

The brain actually has a method of getting us back on track. As psychologists have discovered, even small changes in the way we eat and exercise will create an upward spiral that makes the dopamine receptors in our brain more sensitive, and when they are sensitive, they activate our brain's "reward system." So, although the exercise may seem excruciating in the beginning, it will soon start to get better, and eventually become rewarding, even if that may seem impossible in the beginning.

So work it!

Physical activity works from the inside out. When you feel better physically, it makes you feel better emotionally too. Regular exercises can help you firm up and define your muscles so you look better in your clothes.

Naturally, looking better raises a person's self-esteem, and once we feel good, it's because our system is filled with a rush of "feel good " hormones. This allows us to be able to stay alert, concentrate on schoolwork our jobs. It even makes it easier to deal with relationships.

As we improve our emotional health, we inadvertently improve our self-esteem too. Our interactive skills and social relations also get improved. We will most likely find it easier to talk to people and relate with them because your increased self-confidence. You could also go out and find people who you have common interests with, which would be one of the first few steps you need to take to establish new relationships and develop a better support network.

Chapter Fourteen

Negative Self-Talk

I know firsthand the damage you can suffer from when you indulge in negative self-talk. There were times where I was constantly fighting against my own self. When I would think about food, I would feel a knot in the very pit of my stomach. At times like this, the voices in my head would get super loud, ugly, and mean. However, I stumbled upon something which has helped me immensely improve the relationship I have with my food, and I believe it will help you a lot, too!

What Is Negative Self-Talk?

Negative self-talk is the internal monologue that goes on in our heads which is anything but beneficial to our goals of dealing with emotional eating. Sometimes it goes on on such a subliminal level that we're almost unaware of it! Usually, all this chatter in our heads is a collection of all sorts of opinions and judgments we've heard or read somewhere, when we were kids. Sometimes it can be tied in to culture, belief, and other people's suggestions, from friends, family, and the media as well. What then happens is sooner or later, we begin to accept what the voice or voices are saying. They begin to color our perception of things, giving us untrue truths we cling onto.

Indulging in Negative Self-Talk

How do you catch yourself thinking these harmful thoughts, if they happen on a level we're barely aware of? Well it's not that hard. See, when you're upset about something, it comes through in the words you say, and how you say those words. Even if you try to mask it by choosing happy sounding words, your body language would be a dead giveaway that something just isn't quite right with you. The same applies with negative-self talk.

There are certain word choices you make in your everyday communication that can clue you in to what your internal monologue is like. Do you say the word "if" a lot? If you use the word "if (like I have in this book a bajillion times, I know, ironic) then what you're implying is that there are conditions to be met, or that there is a possibility whatever you're talking about is not set in stone. It just reeks of uncertainty

So when you say stuff like, "If I start to eat healthy..." Or, "If I manage to lose this weight..." or, "If I finally gain control of my emotions..." What you're really expressing is doubt! You're saying you don't believe you're actually going to achieve any of these things. That's what your self-talk is all about! That's the internal monologue running through your mind, day in, day out.

Why "If"?

Look, you're going to need to take time out and ask yourself why "if" is even in your vocabulary when you're talking about your goals. Take a second, and take a critical look at what possibly erroneous assumptions you have in your mind that would make you use that word in the first place.

Next...

Replace "IF" with "WHEN"

I had to put those in caps for you. There's no ifs, ands, or buts here. So what do you say this time? "When I lose this weight..." or "When I eat healthy..." or "When I gain mastery of my emotions..." See how much more certain and empowering that little word substitution is?

Conditional vs. Definite

See, *If* is a very conditional word. It's also got a huge, negative potential. On the flipside, *When* is a word that says something is **definitely** going to happen, no matter what. It means it's only going to be a matter of time before you finally make it happen. It helps you have a much more positive outlook on your life in general. It immediately silences negative self-talk, and then cranks up the volume on **positive** self-talk. You're reminding yourself that you **can** do this, and you **will**. This is a great way to put you in control.

Which Voice Will You Feed?

Are you going to keep listening to all that internally generated gunk from your mind, or are you going to turn it around, and crank up the volume on the positivity? The choice really is yours. When you allow negative-self talk, it allows you to feel things you really aren't. You become convinced that you're an idiot, and you never achieve anything. You're not sure of success, and a lot surer of failure. You find yourself deliberately lowering your expectations, or even choosing to have none of them to begin with. You arrive at the conclusion that you're not successful, and you're never going to be, because you are completely incapable of success. As a result, you find you have created a self-fulfilling prophecy. You fail, consistently. That's the one thing you win at. Failing.

Honestly, if others could hear your self-talk, would they be appalled? For most people, the answer, sadly, is yes. How do you know for sure you've got really negative internal monologue going on? All you have to do is ask yourself how people would react if they could hear you say it out loud. If you don't want people to hear it, then my friend, you've got some negative self-talk to deal with.

Beating Negative Self-Talk

The only way you're going to be able to deal with this is to become more aware. You need to develop **mindfulness**. Start to pay more attention to what it is you're thinking! Start to think about how you're thinking about things.

As you think about the nature of your thoughts, you'll find you're going to gain some pretty interesting insights to who you are and how your mind works. You'll learn a lot more about the way your mind processes thoughts of food. You'll find your relationship with food to be very revealing, very telling. Once you've got all the revelation, it will become even easier for you to put the new habits we've covered in this book into practice. You will find it much easier to have a better attitude towards your food. You'll find yourself bursting at the seams with ideas and strategies which will help you beat emotional eating, and become the best version of yourself ever!

You've Got The Answers Within

Yes, you do have the answers inside you. You may at this red hot minute not be aware of what those solutions are, but oh boy, they're in there somewhere. I guarantee it. You can take that to the bank and tell the manager I said he should empty the safe for you.

As you become more mindful by observing your thoughts and practicing meditation, you will find that the reasons behind why you eat the way you do will make themselves apparent to you. Once they become clear, it's that much easier for you to change your mind about food. It's easier for you to make a decision about changing up your routines and implementing a healthier lifestyle. You will find it's easier to stick to your commitment to yourself, because you took the time out to go within!

I always recommend my clients practice meditation. It's not only a great way to de-stress and unwind; it can provide some very illuminating insight about your life and the next steps you need to take to make it better, fuller, and richer, too!

Journal

You need a journal. No, it's not a childish thing to have. It's a great way to keep track of your life, and how far you've come. Why? You see it's so easy to lose track of all the progress you've made over time. A journal is great, because you get to see just how far you've come. On days when you're feeling down and out, lost and confused, you can pull out the journal and see how many hurdles you've overcome in the past! If you could overcome them then, then you can overcome them **now.** This will in turn give you such a mighty boost in confidence, and help you dust yourself off and get back on your feet.

A journal is the one place where you can honestly let out all your self-talk. This way, you get to see for yourself what it is you're really thinking. It will teach you what you and food are like in your relationship together. It will show you the beliefs you have gained over time. It will help you understand things you never quite got about yourself, like the impulsive way you eat, and the emotions or events which lead you to eat that way. The journal will hold the key that opens the door to the **real** you. This way, you know what needs to stay, and what needs to go.

As you journal, you're basically gathering a lot of data about yourself. This is data that allows you to take concrete action. Since you now have some solid leads to work with, you can easily uproot all the triggers that make you reach for yet another slice of pizza. Journaling is a surefire way to success.

Discover The Origins of Your Self-Talk

Now, I would be utterly and completely remiss if I did not warn you: this is not going to be a pretty process. When working with clients, I listen to them spew all their negative-self talk. I see them stew in their self-loathing. I'm quick at this time to ask them if they really buy into what they're saying. I'm going to ask you the same thing now:

Do you really believe in all that negative hogwash?

I'm going to go a bit further and ask you this other question:

Would you like to try believing something different?

Usually, this turns on a lightbulb. They realize, "Hey, I don't have to think these thoughts! I'm in charge here! I can choose better feeling thoughts!" And you can, too!

For others, I find we need to dig a little bit deeper so we can discover just where all that negativity first started. We go back to whenever those seeds were planted. Man, I have to tell you the truth: it is no mean feat. Not easy. Not even a little bit. But! It is always completely worth it.

By the time my clients revisit the event - say, some random statement some mean aunt made about their eating habits and their gut at the dinner table - then they're able to see how that was then, and this is now. They're able to see how that mean comment does not have the right to shape their present and future lives. They're able to see how that person's opinions on them no longer matter. It's always a worthwhile endeavor to look for the source of the negative inner monologue.

Action Steps

- First, identify what areas you are facing which pose a major challenge to you. It could be you just can't lay off of the pasta, for example.

- Next, I want you to take your journal, and write about how you feel about pasta. If you've already written about this before, I want you to go through your journal, and explore where your mind went and what it showed you, when you wrote about your dilemma. You might not even have been aware of your pasta issue in the past, and so you may have written nothing about it. That's completely fine. What matters is you now know. It's now in your conscious awareness, which means you can deal with it. So journal about it.

- Next, read through what you've written down now, about pasta. See if it was positive self-talk, or the poopy kind of self-talk. Was it the latter? That's fine. What you should do next is switch it up and make it positive. You could write that you know for a fact that you eat so your body has proper nourishment. Change it up to reflect that you eat not because you're emotionally tied to the food, but because you had a physical desire which needed to be satisfied. Now what this will do is help you rewire your brain, so you only see yourself eating for the right reasons, and act in line with that.

- Now you've modified your self-talk in your journal, brainstorm ideas and strategies that will help you become more conscious of how much pasta you eat daily, and will also help you reduce that amount.

Take Charge of Your Self-Talk!

Don't let negative self-talk take control of your life. Don't let it ruin you to the point where you can't even hear anything positive, and you see no hope for yourself. Don't let it! If that's what you've been doing, take back your power. How? It would help to understand: *You are NOT your mind!* The mind, like the body, is a tool. You are infinity; you are pure energy powering these tools. The energy you put into them is exactly what you'll get back out of them!

Your mind is not unlike your body in this regard: garbage in, garbage out!

CONCLUSION

I know some of what I have said so far may seem a little conflicting. After all how can you love yourself and do what pleases you, when what pleases you is eating like ten bowls of chocolate ice cream and yet maintain a healthy food balance?

I never said it was going to be easy. I am just suggesting you mix a bit of confidence and self-love with a healthy diet. You will be wowed by the results.

Our emotions are very powerful. If we can manage to use positive energy to influence our emotions, we will have really good feelings. Have you ever been around someone at work that seems to always be happy, smiling, talking to people, laughing at every single thing, and you wonder if they ever for any reason feel angry or sad? Well, these people just know how to channel more positive energy.

It's that simple!

Give yourself a reason to laugh or smile. If people don't do it for you, find joy in the little things around you. Spend your time positively. I am sure we all know an idle mind is said to be the devil's workshop! Do not spend idle time contemplating what to eat. Instead, spend it on worthwhile ventures. Everybody has something they have always wanted to do. What's it for you?

It's so easy to blame other people or things for how we are feeling, but people refuse to accept that they are responsible for their emotions. If something makes you mad, talk about it to someone. If you can't, gear up, go to the gym with the picture of the person who made you mad, imagine giving them much needed lessons on boxing.

Find an outlet!

Emotional eating in a lot of people is born from repressed emotions. Some people feel crying makes them look weak. Others feel like calling people out on their crap might hurt the person's feelings. So does this mean it's okay for you to be hurt and just suffer in silence? *No way!*

Go on up to that person and say, "Hey you, I do not like what you said. Kindly offer an apology." If they won't give it, learn to accept that and be okay without it. If you know you were also in the wrong, apologize first. That way, they are more likely to tender an honest apology, and when they do? Forgive them and move on.

Forgiveness is not for them. It's for you! It's just a fancy name for unshackling yourself from a particular issue.

Whatever you're going through, be proactive about finding joy, whether you recently suffered a breakup, you just lost your job or a loved one, someone called you Fatty NcFatterson... It' doesn't matter! Know you are perfect. You deserve to be loved. You especially deserve love from **you.** I'm willing to bet there is someone out there who is dying to meet you! He or she is probably praying every night to have you in their lives. You just haven't met them yet. So, put yourself out there, interact, socialize and you might just get a step closer to meeting your better half.

Ah! The smell of potential love is in the air!

You need emotions to survive. Don't try to suppress them. Find healthy ways to express them. Let them out and let them go. Don't bury it all deep down inside till you start feeling emotional hunger again.
.
Take the wheel of your life, and drive! Drive responsibly. Imagine your emotions are a new Bugatti you just bought. Of course you would drive carefully and avoid leaving scratches on your new baby!

Handle your emotions with just as much attention and care!

Nurture them, direct them, take care of them, and do not let them get you into trouble. Because unruly emotions bring about emotional eating, along with health complications and other eating disorders.

Love Yourself

You have to learn to love yourself so others can love you. It doesn't matter if you have a good sized stomach or a generous behind. There is this aura confident people who love themselves give off.

Have you ever walked beside someone and thought to yourself this person feels good about themselves? We usually think that because this person walks ramrod straight with a pep in their step and the wind in their hair. It's not just what you are seeing. It's what they believe about themselves that you see and feel! That's the energy they are giving off, and you just can't help but really sense it. If you look closely, you might see a zit or two, even a mole somewhere. But it doesn't matter because that self-love and confidence they exude just blinds you to all that. So be that guy!

Feel good about yourself! If only you knew how many people in the world want to be like you. Someone somewhere is tired of being too skinny or too short or tall, while you want to be as skinny or as whatever as they are. It's human nature to want what we can't or don't have. It's even taught in economics that humans are insatiable. You might wish you were skinny now, but if you actually were, you would understand the struggles of a skinny person. Appreciate what you have now because someone somewhere wants it.

Everyone Is Unique

We are all unique beings. Our genes and environment play a huge role in how we look. You can't come from a family of generously proportioned people and expect to be as thin as a reed. Not without doing some work! Accept what you are, and do what you can to change it to what you prefer. You don't have to loathe yourself along the way to change.

Emotional eating is an issue. A big one.

if you feel you are an emotional eater but you aren't really sure, talk to someone who listens and might understand. If you are for any reason too shy for that, you could dedicate a little of time to research. Try to check what level of seriousness yours has gotten to. If it is quite serious, try to see an expert. Do not do anything drastic.

We all have problems. We have things that may keep wide awake late into the night; things that cause us to worry, fear, or push us to anger. It's how we deal with these things that matter.

For example, you may have lost your job. See it as a new opportunity to further your career.
Did you really mean to work for someone else for the rest of your life, anyway? There are many opportunities out there. You could come up with something new, or if you can't, follow one of the many job trends out there. Just try to be a bit innovative. Who knows, you might be the change we have all been looking forward to!

Be Easy About This
The problem is we try to conform to a certain structure. We are all afraid of exploring and trying new things, because we are afraid to fail.

Well, you won't know until you try! So try!

So what if you fall flat on your face when you begin working on your emotional eating issues? Pick yourself up and start again. Just because you stepped out of line once or twice in a row doesn't mean you should call it quits. Stop being so hard on yourself!

Explore The New

Do you love to dance but really don't know how? Why not go for dancing lessons then? It's a form of exercise and it helps keep your mind occupied.

Travel somewhere else and learn about their culture and practices. It's never too late to learn something new! You don't always have to limit your travels to the images in a travel book.

Deal With It

The best way of dealing with situations is to meet them head on. Try strategic methods of approach.

Or, if you know they are not important at all and unnecessarily bothering you, then forget it! Some problems just come to challenge your resolve. You don't have to let that one thing win. Don't let it drag you under and push you into unhealthy habits.

Live! Love! Learn!

Every waking moment is a learning experience, so be open to new opportunities. Be a willing student of life. There is no limit to learning. When you are engaged in productive activities, time seems to fly by in a blur. You won't even have time for unhealthy eating habits.

As long as you live, there are better options and opportunities out there. You haven't even tried one-third of them yet, so how can you claim to be bored? Have you read every novel, magazine or comic there is? Or listened to every song ever sung? Or participated in every game known to man?

You, my dear, have no excuse.

The only thing you can do for yourself is to live a good, and healthy life. You will be grateful for it in your old age.

So, grab opportunities and live the best life you can.

31007613R00106

Printed in Great
Britain
by Amazon